SAIN' the JOURNEY

INSPIRING LIVES FROM EVERY AGE

JOHN MURRAY

First published in 2017 by Messenger Publications

ISBN 978 1 910248 33 1

Designed by Messenger Publications Design Department
Typeset in Trajan and Baskerville
Printed by W&G Baird Ltd

MESSENGER
PUBLICATIONS
JESUITS in IRELAND

Messenger Publications,
37 Lower Leeson Street, Dublin 2
www.messenger.ie

Introduction

Countless posters of celebrities from pop culture, or the worlds of sport and entertainment, may adorn many walls today, but the people in these posters will probably never know who it is that is trying to emulate them.

This is not the case with saints! They too provide a model for us, but more than that, they can support us in our efforts, through their prayer of intercession on our behalf. That is why in a Litany of Saints, we ask individual saints to 'pray for us'.

These saints can arrive in our lives by all sorts of routes; perhaps by Christian names given to us at baptism, or maybe by the name we choose for ourselves at confirmation.

Of course not all saints are officially named so. As I grow older, I find an increasing encouragement for the celebration the unnamed saints – All Saints Day (1 November) and All the Saints of Ireland (6 November) being prime examples. These people became saints by facing the same situations that you and I face everyday and, admittedly, making a better job of it!

Fr John Murray has always shown a great talent and aptitude for selecting saints from across the centuries and from other countries, and seeing in their lifestyles those qualities that would be helpful for us in our lives. I am so pleased that Fr John has made available here a second allocation of those insights, following his *Saints of our Time*, for you and me to enjoy.

So, alongside the named saints in the Litany of Saints, we add a further prayer: 'All holy men and women, pray for us'.

Bishop Anthony Farquhar,
Emeritus Auxiliary Bishop of Down and Connor.

CONTENTS

CONTENTS

ANGELA MERICI
(1474~1540)

'It was the best of times; it was the worst of times.' Readers will undoubtedly recognise these words as the first line of Dickens's *A Tale of Two Cities*. It is a line that many could embrace for their own times and in their own lands. Might we apply these words to Ireland now? There is a new challenge to the gospel, here and elsewhere, and those who follow Christ are called to work out new ways of doing so. Such was the situation of Angela Merici, who was born in 1474 in Desenzano del Garda in Northern Italy. She herself was orphaned at an early age and, in addition, lost a sister.

It was a time when there were few choices for young girls and women in either society or the Church. While the world was changing in many ways, with the new culture of the Renaissance challenging people to think differently about society and the Church, for young women there remained only two choices: to marry or to enter a convent. Convent life entailed a cloistered existence: the whole idea of apostolic religious women, involved in schools or other activities, was unheard of. It took women like Angela Merici and Catherine of Siena in the previous century to pioneer a new way for women to live the gospel.

From an early age Angela was privileged to enjoy the gift of visions. Shortly after her sister died, she had a vision in which her sister's salvation was assured. As a result, Angela became a Franciscan tertiary and began to adopt a life of prayer and simplicity in keeping with that great founder's charism. As part of her prayer life, she visited the many shrines of Italy, and even undertook to go to the Holy Land. However, before arriving there, she was mysteriously struck blind and ended up seeing nothing. Her sight returned at the very end of the pilgrimage. The motif of sight or vision appears again later, when she had a vision in which she saw a company of angels and young women descending from a ladder in the heavens. A voice revealed that she would one day create a new community of women whose numbers would be as many as the women in the vision.

Like Catherine of Siena some decades before her, Angela's life was not just about prayer. She had been touched by the lack of education for girls in her neighbourhood, and had undertaken to provide some basic religious instruction for them. Over the years, when she was not travelling, she made this her regular occupation. And, as with so many great religious founders, others were attracted by her witness and began to join her. One thinks in Ireland, for instance, of Edmund Rice and the Christian Brothers, and Nano Nagle and the Presentation sisters. In 1533, when Angela was in her late fifties, she set about formalising this new gathering of women. Two years later she had a group of twenty-eight women around her, and they took as their patron St Ursula, a fourth-century martyr who was popularly venerated as a protector of women.

The following year Angela laid down the rules of the Ursulines, clarifying her plans to restore the family and the richness of Christianity through the education of girls. 'Disorder in society is the result of disorder in the family', she wrote. Yet, although Angela devised a rule for her sisters, she did not think of them as a religious order. They did not wear a religious habit, as other women of the time did. They took no vows, and generally they continued to live with their families and not behind an enclosure or convent wall. The idea of such an association was unheard of at that time, and it aroused certain concerns among the Church authorities. Nevertheless, the work of Angela and her sisters in educating the poor girls of the region was greatly admired and valued. The teaching of the Reformers had made great inroads into the traditional faith of the people of Brescia by the time of Angela's death. However, her sisters were able to redress this balance in the decades that followed and restore and strengthen Catholicism in her native Italy.

In due course, Angela was chosen as the association's first superior. She used this position to devote herself to the spiritual formation of the increasing number of women who were attracted by the group's charism and zeal. In Brescia she was revered as a living saint, and often crowds would follow her as she made her way to the church for Mass. No doubt there were those who followed her out of mere curiosity, but there were many others who were attracted by her simple holiness and her quiet witness to the values of Christ and of St Francis.

She died on 27 January 1540 after a long illness, and was buried in the ancient church of St Afra (now St Angela's sanctuary) where she still rests. Just four years later the Church, through Pope Paul III, approved a constitution for her religious community, which would in time number many thousands of women. Angela was beatified in 1768 and canonised by Pope Pius VII in 1807. Her body remains incorrupt. The sisters of the order and their many alumnae throughout the world not so long ago celebrated the 475th anniversary of their foundation.

ANTONI GAUDÍ
(1852~1926)

Barcelona! The very name is inspirational. For those who love football it evokes 'the beautiful game', and a visit to Camp Nou is essential for any fan. Yet, in a city of nearly two million people, it is not the skyscrapers or the football stadiums which dominate the skyline, but a church dedicated to the Holy Family, which has been well over a hundred years in the making and is still not finished! The Basilica of La Sagrada Familia was started in the nineteenth century and should be completed by the year 2050. It may sound incredible to us today, but 100 years from now we can be sure that the name of its architect, Antoni Gaudí, will be better known than that of Lionel Messi in this city, to which the former has given so much beauty and the latter such great joy.

The most famous architect of the twentieth century was born in Reus in the Tarragona province of Catalonia, eighty kilometres south of Barcelona. After enduring a childhood troubled by rheumatism, this son of coppersmiths travelled to the Catalan capital to enrol as a student at the Escola Tècnica Superior d'Arquitectura, where he duly studied from 1873 to 1877. Even then his professors did not quite know what to make of his work, such was its originality, and when he was awarded the title of architect in 1878, Elies Rogent, the director of the school, declared, 'Who knows if we have given this diploma to a nut or to a genius? Time will tell.'

Well, time has shown that 'genius' was the correct word. Between 1984 and 2005, seven of Gaudí's works were declared World Heritage sites by UNESCO. Driven by his passion for his native Catalonia, his love of nature and, above all, his love for his faith, Gaudí left behind many wonderful and exciting buildings in his beloved city and the surrounding areas. To be fair to his professor, however, it is important to note that as a student Gaudí obtained mostly average grades and that he occasionally failed courses. Perhaps here is a lesson for all teachers to try to recognise the pearl within the dull shell sitting before them!

To some people, Gaudí's life may seem strange, but like many artists he was totally involved in his work. Apparently he was attracted to only one woman, a teacher named Josefa, but the attraction was not reciprocated. Thereafter he took refuge in his Catholic faith, which remained central to him throughout the rest of his life. He was a devout man, and frequently, almost daily, attended Mass before beginning his day's work.

Among the many extraordinary buildings Gaudí designed, it is above all the great Basilica of the Holy Family with which he will always be most closely associated. Pope Benedict XVI visited Barcelona on 7 November 2010 and dedicated the church and the altar, something which was unusual since they were incomplete at the time. Originally the church had been the brainchild of a group called the Devotees of St Joseph, and the theme of Joseph, the foster father of Jesus and husband of Mary, features strongly throughout. The hope of those who inspired the church was to remind the world at that time of the value of love, work and service lived in the presence of God. In his sermon given during the Mass of Dedication, Pope Benedict remarked that Gaudí, when faced by many seemingly impossible problems with the construction, would state, 'St Joseph will finish this church'.

Elsewhere in that same sermon, Pope Benedict said, 'The genius of Antoni Gaudí, inspired by the ardour of his Christian faith, succeeded in raising this sanctuary as a hymn of praise to God carved in stone. As with the birth of Christ, this hymn of praise has had as its protagonists the most humble and simple of people. In effect, Gaudí, through his work, sought to bring the gospel to everyone. For this reason, he conceived of the three porticos of the exterior of the church as a catechesis on the life of Jesus Christ, as a great rosary, which is the prayer of ordinary people, a prayer in which are contemplated the joyful, sorrowful and glorious mysteries of our Lord.'

Continuing to speak of Gaudí, Pope Benedict added: 'In collaboration with the parish priest, Gil Parés, he also designed and financed from his own savings the creation of a school for the children of the workers and of the poorest families in the neighbourhood, which was at that time an outlying suburb of Barcelona. He brought concrete reality to the conviction saying, "The poor must always find a welcome in the Church, which is an expression of Christian charity".'

In his youth, Gaudí liked his costly suits and his well-groomed hair and beard. He enjoyed the trappings of his profession and his increasing fame. But the older Gaudí – being more conscious of gospel simplicity and totally absorbed in his project – lived frugally, dressed shabbily and neglected his appearance, so much so that when he was knocked down by a tram in 1926 no one recognised him. By the time the chaplain of the Sagrada Familia came it was too late for any serious medical intervention. He died on 10 June at the age of seventy-three, and was buried two days later. A huge crowd attended the funeral, which took place in the crypt of the great basilica which he had begun to build.

The cause of Gaudí's beatification was introduced in Rome in the mid-nineties, and about ten years later 'God's architect', as he has been called, was proclaimed a 'Servant of God', the first stage on the way to sainthood. Saints, however, like beautiful churches, can some-times take a long time to come to completion. If anyone is surprised at the length of time the Sagrada Familia is taking to complete, it is worth remembering Gaudí's own response to the delays that he encountered to his great work: 'My client can wait'. Saints too are made in God's time, not ours.

In October 2015 Pope Francis, the Synod of Bishops and certain advisors – women and married couples among them – gathered in Rome to pray and reflect on the role of the family in the New Evangelisation. Since then, Pope Francis has published his profound and challenging reflections on the family in the apostolic exhortation *Amoris Laetitia*. For the pope, the family is above all a great gift from God, to be cherished and celebrated by all believers. Let us pray that our families may be lasting monuments to our loving God, just as Gaudí's great masterpiece draws up upward in prayer and gratitude to the Father of us all.

BERNADETTE SOUBIROUS
(1844~1879)

It is almost 160 years since an obscure town in the Pyrenees Mountains of Southern France became a household name for Catholics all
over the world. On 11 February 1858, Bernadette Soubirous, aged
fourteen, was minding sheep with a sister and a friend when she saw
what she termed 'a small young lady' standing in a niche in the rock
at Massabielle, near the town of Lourdes. The other two saw nothing,
but Bernadette was to return there on seventeen occasions for meet-
ings with 'the beautiful lady'.

The story of Lourdes and Bernadette's visions is well documented.
The Lady did not identify herself until the seventeenth meeting, but
from early on, many of the townsfolk began to accompany the girl
to her meeting with 'the Lady', whom they assumed was the Virgin
Mary. On the thirteenth meeting she was told 'to go to the priests and
tell them to build a chapel here'.

Bernadette, accompanied by two of her aunts, went to the local
parish priest, Fr Dominique Peyramale. He was a good priest, but
he did not want to encourage any 'pious fanaticism' in his parish.
So he asked the Lady for a sign: to make the rose bush beneath the
niche bud and flower, even though it was the middle of February. This
happened. When the priest later asked Bernadette to get the Lady
to identify herself, the answer, given in the local patois, was *'Que soy*

era Immaculada Concepciou' – 'I am the Immaculate Conception'. The expression was certainly one unknown to a simple, undereducated peasant girl, and one which relatives said she would never have heard before. Pope Pius IX had promulgated this dogma of Our Lady only four years earlier, in 1854. Despite rigorous investigation by officials of both the Church and the French government, Bernadette stuck to her story over the following months and years. Indeed, her behaviour during this period set an example by which all who claim visions and mystical experiences are now judged by Church authorities.

Her request for a chapel to be built was in time granted, and the sanctuary at Lourdes was to become one of the major Catholic pilgrimage sites in the world. It is reckoned that nearly 5,000 healings or miracles have taken place there, but the Church – rigorous, as always, in its assessment – has recognised only sixty-seven.

As for Bernadette herself, she was beatified in 1925 and canonised by Pope Pius XI in 1933. Her feast day is 16 April. Her body had been exhumed on two occasions before this (in 1909 and 1919) and was found not to have decomposed. This was taken as one of the indications of her sanctity in support of the canonisation. However, it was her humility that was probably the greatest factor in raising her to the altars.

When the apparitions were over, life could never be the same for Bernadette. She was constantly pestered by the countless pilgrims who were beginning to come to Lourdes, and on the advice of Fr Peyramale, she decided to enter a convent. There were many offers from all over France, but in the end she chose the Sisters of Charity of Nevers. And so Bernadette, at age twenty-two, entered the convent in the year 1866. Before leaving home, however, she went for the last time to the grotto to bid farewell and to ask for help. Her parting from her parents was particularly sad, as she knew that she would never see them again. Both would die within a few short years of her entering.

The sisters at Nevers were pleased to receive their new 'little saint', yet things did not begin too well. The mistress of novices, Mother Marie Thérèse Vauzou, was looking forward to meeting her new postulant and to accompanying her in her early days in religious life, but their first contact was awkward: Bernadette was not as well educated as the older sister and was unable to respond to her questioning. The mistress was embarrassed, and from that day on was openly distrustful of the new arrival.

Bernadette knew she wasn't stupid, but in those early days her thoughts kept going back to the bishop's parting words when, in an interview with him, she wondered what she could offer to the convent. 'You can help in the kitchen,' was his reply, 'cutting carrots.' The occasional humiliations over the ensuing years were borne with humility and patience by the young sister. Her health too became poor. She had contracted cholera when she was eleven, and this, wedded to the poor nutrition of a peasant family, meant that she was always in poor health. Indeed, the last three years of her relatively short life were spent as an invalid.

The pain of tuberculosis devoured Bernadette, but she never lost her humour or her concern for the other sisters. In the end, when death came, she asked for a crucifix which had been a gift from Pope Pius IX. She took it in her hands and slowly kissed the wounds of Christ, one by one. Then, at precisely the hour Jesus died, she too expired, with the words, 'Holy Mary, Mother of God, pray for me, poor sinner, poor sinner...'

When the news reached the streets of Nevers, spontaneous shouts went up, 'The saint is dead! The saint is dead!' The local people knew the worth of the gentle nun who had lived within their town's borders. Many of them had seen their prayers granted through her intercession. Today, hundreds of thousands of pilgrims visit this pre-eminent shrine of Mary. The name of the town is synonymous with healing and prayer and Mary. The little girl with no special airs or graces will be particularly pleased that 'her Lady' is so honoured.

COLUMBAN
(543~615)

The Church is often strong, even if it seems poor in outward appearance. It is strong when it begins to look outside itself, to share its blessings, to manifest its concern for others. The Church is weaker when it tries – perhaps unconsciously – to preserve itself, to maintain its position, to protect its privileges. The first Church – the apostles in the Upper Room after the death of Jesus, trying perhaps to protect themselves – needed to be blown out by the power of the Holy Spirit on Pentecost day.

Within a generation of St Patrick's mission (432-461), the Church in Ireland was firmly established. Thousands converted to the new faith. Kings, chieftains and their people were enthusiastic in their commitment. Monasteries began to be established all over the land, and for centuries Ireland was justifiably called 'the island of saints and scholars'.

Within a short time, missionaries began to spread eastward to Britain and on to the continent of Europe. Irish monks played a major part in stabilising the volatile civilisation of the continent, which at that time was constantly under threat from the various pagan tribes, such as the Vandals, the Huns and the Goths. Their monasteries became safe havens for precious manuscripts and artworks, though they sometimes proved an attraction for the marauding invaders too.

One of the greatest of these missionaries was Columban. His name in Irish – *Columbán*, which means 'White Dove' – is sometimes given in its Latin form, *Columbanus*. He was born in 543 to a prosperous family in Meath. Prior to his birth, his mother had a premonition that the child she would bear would be 'a remarkable genius'. What mother doesn't have secret dreams for her children? Columban's background enabled him to be well educated and trained in the various disciplines of the age: grammar, rhetoric, geometry and, of course, the Sacred Scriptures.

Perhaps his family had worldly dreams for him but, like the great St Benedict before him, Columban resisted the attractions and temptations he saw all around and fled to a monastery – first to Cluaninis in Lough Erne and then to Bangor on the northern arm of present-day County Down. There he lived for many years, a diligent and zealous monk until, in the year 585 when he was already in his forties, he was inspired to reverse the missionary venture of Patrick and to carry the faith back to Europe. With the blessing of the great abbot Comgall, Columban set sail for Gaul – France today – with twelve companions, and set up a monastery in Burgundy. This foundation quickly attracted such large numbers that several others had to be established in the area under the authority of Columban. As well as the great numbers who wished to join these communities there were many others who simply came on pilgrimage. Columban himself always sought greater solitude, however, spending periods of time in a hermitage. Often he would withdraw to a cave several miles away, accompanied only by a single companion who acted as a messenger to the other monks and to the outside world.

If you are living according to the gospel, people will either join you or persecute you. Columban knew both reactions. Despite a growing popularity with many young people who were attracted by the radical simplicity of his lifestyle, Columban came in for criticism from some of the local bishops who disagreed with him over the date of Easter. This was a sometimes contentious issue in the early Church, and the Irish practice differed from that of Gaul. As well as that, many of the bishops thought Columban's spirituality to be too severe. In time, the more benign rule of St Benedict would prevail in religious life in the West. But that is another story.

The disagreement with the bishops was basically about influence, and Columban, as the outsider, was bound to lose. In a letter he wrote to them, his words are particularly poignant: 'I came as a poor stranger into these parts for the cause of Christ, our Saviour. One thing alone I ask of you, holy Fathers, permit me to live in silence in these forests, near the bones of seventeen of my brethren now dead.'

Columban also ran foul of the local royal family. When the King, Theuderic of Burgundy, began living with a mistress, Columban refused to baptise the sons who were born to the union. Strangely, like the bible story of Herod and John the Baptist, Theuderic liked to come and listen to Columban, but it was the king's grandmother who schemed to have Columban removed from the area. In 610 he, along with the other native Irish monks, was taken to Nantes under armed escort, there to await a ship to return them to Ireland.

A storm prevented the ship from setting out, however, and Columban with his remaining monks somehow escaped and sailed up the Rhine, hoping to settle in the area around Lake Constance. Sadly, there too he encountered opposition. It seems that Europe's current indifference and hostility to the faith are not new! Then, as now, the preacher needed to be reminded of St Paul's words to his young charge Timothy: 'Preach the gospel in season and out of season, welcome or unwelcome' *(2 Tm.4:2)*. Despite the setback, Columban remained undaunted. He shook the dust off his feet and moved on. Everywhere he went he established new settlements and places of prayer and study. Finally, he arrived and settled in Bobbio in Northern Italy, where he founded his most famous abbey in 614.

Columban's time in Bobbio was to be short – he died in 615. However, as elsewhere, his life there was to be full and eventful. In contrast to Burgundy, he was warmly welcomed by the local royalty. The Queen, Theodelinda, played an important part in restoring Nicene Christianity in that area, against the prevailing heresy of Arianism which, though condemned in 325 at the great Council of Nicaea, had never gone away. Theodelinda engaged Columban, with his wisdom and learning, in this enterprise. It is a testimony to the saint's influence that fourteen centuries later there are at least thirty-four parishes in the area surrounding Bobbio called by his name. He has been remembered closer to home as well of course. Almost a century ago, the great Society of St Columban was founded by Frs Edward Galvin and John Blowick to bring the gospel to the nations of the world, in imitation of the great saint. Its work continues to this day.

We have recently celebrated a special anniversary of St Columban's death, with events in Ireland, Bobbio and other places associated with the saint. May we allow the Holy Spirit – as he did for Columban – to blow us out of our 'upper rooms'.

DAMIEN OF MOLOKAI
(1840~1889)

He knew immediately that he had made a mistake. The man with the gangrenous hand had come forward for communion. Damien looked at it for a few seconds and then dropped the host into the putrid mass of flesh. There was a moment of silence. The man looked at Damien without expression. Then the priest gently lifted the host and placed it again in the man's hand. The young priest had received the gift of mercy.

The journey of Damien De Veuster began years before this in his native country of Belgium, where he was born in 1840 and given the baptismal name Joseph. Belgium at that time had a strong Catholic and missionary tradition. Two of his sisters became nuns, and one brother a priest. Following this brother's example, the young Joseph joined the Congregation of the Sacred Hearts, where he took the name Damien. After completing his training, he set sail for the islands of Hawaii – replacing of his brother who had taken ill – and was ordained in the city of Honolulu in May 1864.

Because of its frequent use in Bible stories relating to Jesus, we are familiar to an extent with the term 'leper'. Since time immemorial, leprosy has been one of the most feared diseases of all. Unfortunate lepers had to keep their distance from the community in order not to further spread the disease. They lived apart from others, and if they walked the roads they had to shout out loud, 'unclean, unclean', so that others could avoid their path and their smell. Today, thanks to modern medicine, leprosy has a name – Hansen's disease – but, more importantly, treatment is now available which has greatly removed it as the scourge which afflicted so many in the past.

Back now to the story of Damien. When westerners arrived in the Hawaiian Islands at the end of the eighteenth century they found a population of about 300,000. Yet, within a few decades, that population had been severely reduced. The local people were not immune to the different germs and viruses which the newcomers brought. The worst of these was leprosy.

The first case of leprosy occurred in 1840, the year of Damien's birth. Within the following thirty years, however, the disease reached epidemic proportions. In 1866, the authorities reacted by establishing a leper settlement on the island of Molokai, which was remote and somewhat inaccessible. By law, those who were found to be suffering from the disease were removed by force from their families and brought to this place of exile. It was a cruel fate. From 1866 to 1969 a total of about 8,000 Hawaiians were sent to the peninsula for medical quarantine.

Initially conditions were horrendous. People were literally dumped on the shore of the island, left to make their own way inland to find shelter in caves or makeshift shacks. They had to search for food and try to get on with the others who had already been assigned a similar fate. There was no government, no civil law or moral code. People were simply left to their own devices.

During the early years of his priesthood, the young Damien worked on the largest island of Hawaii, before spending further years on the islands of Kohala and Hamakua. They were happy years of ministry among a beautiful people, lived against a backdrop of spectacular scenery. But the young man was aware of the leper colony on

Molokai, and he shared with his friends his undeniable feeling that he should join them. On one occasion he wrote to his brother, 'I make myself a leper to gain all to Jesus Christ'. He said this several years before he contracted the disease himself.

In 1873, he got his wish when, with Bishop Louis Maigret of the same order, he landed at Kalaupapa on the island of Molokai. Making coffins for the dead and building houses for the living were among his earliest tasks. He started building small chapels too, in order to give a sense of dignity to these people whom society had rejected. Soon the young priest was going from leper to leper, washing and bandaging each one. His limited medical skills were more than matched by his charity and his increasing view of the lepers as individuals worthy of respect and kindness. 'I have seen him', said a visitor, 'dress the most loathsome sores as if he were arranging flowers.'

Restoring dignity was at the heart of Damien's mission of mercy. For the sports-loving Hawaiians he organised races, even though some competitors had lost their feet. He also formed a choir and a band, and engaged two organists who had ten fingers between them to play at the funeral Masses, of which, sadly, there were many.

One morning, as Damien was washing his own feet, he moved the soapy cloth slowly over his toes and realised that he was feeling nothing. He knew the signs. When he next preached at Mass, Damien was able to begin with the words, 'We lepers'. The year was 1884, and although the disease had begun in his left foot it spread quickly to other parts of his body, bringing about an increasing paralysis and eventually death on 15 April 1889. He was forty-nine.

Some decades later, in 1936, at the request of King Leopold III and the Belgian Government, his body was returned to his own land, and he was buried in his native town of Leuven. After his beatification in 1995, however, the remains of his right hand, with which he had tended and blessed so many, were returned to Molokai and reinterred in the original grave, beneath a pandanus tree where he had first slept when he arrived on the island. Pope Benedict XVI canonised this much-loved saint in 2009. A statue of the leper priest stands today in Washington DC, representing the State of Hawaii. The marks he bore on his body were those of Jesus.

Elvira Petrozzi
(b.1937)

I watched the elderly nun march purposefully across the yard. Coming towards her was a young man who was tall and well built. He was wearing work clothes and he was covered in dust. Yet when they met he gave her a great bear-hug like some long-lost friend. 'Isn't that Sr Elvira?' I said to a young man nearby. 'Isn't she the foundress?' 'Yes, it is; she is our mother; she is number one!' he replied.

To visit a Cenacle (*Cenacolo* in Italian) is a beautiful experience. It is to enter into another world where the hardness of the world is left behind and dreams are allowed to be fashioned. The Cenacolo Community was founded by Sr Elvira Petrozzi, an Italian nun, in 1983. For many years she had been concerned by the destruction she had seen among young people through drug abuse, and she longed to help them. Since she had no formal training to work with addicts, and since the charism of her order was teaching, it was eight years before she managed to persuade her superiors that this was a genuine call from God and to release her for this work.

Elvira began with two companions: a fellow religious, Sr Aurelia, and a lay teacher, Nives Grato. They begged for and obtained an old abandoned house in the city of Saluzzo in Italy, for which she had to pay the sum of one dollar a year to the local council. On 16 July, the feast of Our Lady of Mount Carmel, the Cenacle Community was born. Sr Elvira said that a priest who had come to stay with them suggested this name and she liked it. She thought of the upper room in Jerusalem where the disciples went after the crucifixion of Jesus out of fear. So many young people were full of fear, with so much loneliness and restlessness in their hearts.

Soon young people began arriving having heard of someone who wanted to help them in their desperation. Elvira began to care for them, but it was a steep learning curve! In the beginning the young drug addicts were allowed to smoke and even have a glass of wine – as Italians do – with their meal. But one night she returned to the house to find that all the young men in the community were drunk, having bored a hole in the kitchen wall in order to finish off the supplies of wine! So alcohol – and in time tobacco too – were banned from the communities, decisions that were made by the young people themselves.

While secular detox programmes will use drug substitutes to wean people off drugs, Sr Elvira had a different approach. Many of these young people had tried to cope with their problems by turning to drugs. Their often-selfish focus was simply the next "fix". She wanted to show them that there was a much better way, and that way was Christ. Thus the Cenacle Community was not so much a drug rehabilitation centre as a school of life with prayer at its heart. To many it seemed initially like a spiritual boot camp, where they learned to live in a totally new way. Instead of relying on the crutch of drugs to escape from everything that was painful, they learned to accept a simple lifestyle and to rediscover the gifts of work and friendship and faith in the Word of God. Through the work of the Cenacle the addicts learned to embrace the suffering and pain they found in their lives and give it to Jesus in prayer, especially before the Blessed Sacrament.

One of the most important roles within the Cenacle, which Elvira developed, was that of the 'guardian angels', who are fellow addicts further along the spiritual journey than newcomers. They offer emotional and spiritual support to the young addict who may have just entered the community and is struggling to cope. The 'angels' provide 24/7 support in terms of listening and encouraging, even making cups of tea for their young charges during the night. This unconditional love melts the hardest of hearts, and helps prepare the newcomer for the day when they too will be able to do the same for others.

In time many return to normal society and get jobs, and eventually a spouse and family. But others remain in the Cenacle to help others who have arrived at that same point they were at perhaps just a year or two before. Many married couples have been formed out of friendships forged in the Cenacle, though the boys and girls have separate communities. And – beautifully – a new religious order has grown up within the community from former addicts.

Today there are over sixty-six Cenacles throughout the world, with the majority in Italy. Their number is still growing. There is a Cenacle now in Ireland at Knock, which opened on the feast of the Immaculate Conception in 1999. For Sr Elvira her dream has come true, and she is living to see it bear so much fruit around the world.

In October 2005 Pope Benedict honoured Sr Elvira by inviting her to be present as an auditor at the Synod on the Eucharist. Her own deep faith in the Eucharist is perhaps the greatest reason for the success of the Cenacles. While attending the Synod she shared her convictions and her faith with the Fathers: 'The Eucharist is nourishment, much more filling than pasta or food for the body. The Eucharist is reconciliation, encounter, amazement, beauty, strength, risk. It gives you everything that you need to live each day, and it makes you learn so many things.' With such faith in the Eucharist, the Cenacle has become a place of healing for many people, a place where new dreams are made possible.

ÈVE LAVALLIÈRE
(1866~1929)

The story of Ève Lavallière is a story of grace triumphing over sin and circumstance. It is a story of hope for anyone whose life seems to be a mess and out of control. Above all, it is a story of mercy: the mercy of God, the 'Hound of Heaven' who seeks out the lost sheep, even those who want to be lost and never found. Ève (her real name was Eugénie Marie Pascaline Fenoglio) was to go on to become a great actress on the French stage, but her family beginnings were far from happy.

Born in 1866 in Toulon in the south of France, Ève experienced a turbulent childhood, mainly due to her father. He was a tailor, but also an alcoholic who was frequently unfaithful to his wife. Often he would beat her and his rages would terrorise the household. In desperation, Eve's mother would then take her daughter and son away to relatives, but would always return when her husband begged her to do so.

Respite came for young Ève when she was sent to a boarding school, where she received kindness and understanding. She also had moments of spiritual joy, especially when she made her First Holy Communion. It was an anticipation of things to come. At this stage too, the signs of her future career began to make themselves known. Often she would organise her friends into a theatre group and she herself would write little plays and songs for them – even designing the costumes and sets herself.

However, real tragic drama was to occur all too soon in the family setting. Unable to endure the torment any more, her mother finally decided to leave her husband for good, taking her children with her. Her husband followed them and, in a moment of violent rage, shot his wife dead and then killed himself. In the aftermath of his tragedy, Ève went to live from one from relative to another, hoping for security and support. By this time, she had abandoned the faith of her childhood, and found herself full of despair and even close to suicide.

She then fell into the welcoming arms of a stranger who recognised her theatrical talents and invited her to join a theatre group. The sudden death of one of the leading actresses of the theatre proved to be an opportunity for Ève, and she did not disappoint. She had an exceptional voice, which she was able to use to convey every sort of emotion – from sadness to anger, from authority to disgust. Listening to Ève transported the audience into the very heart of whatever she was playing, whether tragedy or comedy. The great contemporary actress, Sarah Bernhardt, paid her the following compliment: 'What you do is innate. You create – you do not copy the characters. You give birth to them from within yourself. It is very beautiful.'

At this time Ève also became the mistress of a local marquis. It was he who changed her name to Ève Lavallière – she often wore a tie which at that time was known as the 'Lavallière tie' – to avoid detection by her family. Ironically, Vallière was also the name of a mistress of King Louis XIV, who ended her days as a Carmelite nun! Gifts and luxuries were now the order of the day as, after her performances, Ève held court in some of the most fashionable restaurants in Paris.

Eventually she left the marquis, only to fall in love with a theatrical director with whom she had a child. This man, however, was far from faithful, and he had several other relationships with women. For her part, Ève was also enjoying liaisons with a variety of men who rewarded her sexual favours. She also enjoyed the attention of the critics who considered her performances, in musical comedy especially, to be beyond compare. In her time, Ève was as famous in France as many Hollywood actresses are today. She was the *belle dame* of the Paris stage; often she acted before the kings and queens of Europe as they visited the French capital.

Yet, off-stage, Eve was miserable. Despite the fame, money and popular acclaim, her life continued to spiral out of control. She had everything, and yet was deeply unhappy. Three times she resolved to kill herself; each time deciding against it at the last moment.

Then, one summer, she was on holiday in a French village called Chanceaux-sur-Choisille in the east of France. There she met the local parish priest, Fr Chasteigner, who invited her to Mass. At this stage she was well enough known in France for the priest to know the sort of person she had become. She attended Mass, but later told the priest that she had made a pact with the Devil in exchange for twenty more years of youthfulness. Fr Chasteigner was shocked, and immediately told her she must repent. It was a moment of grace for her: suddenly she realised that if the devil existed so must God, and that she ought to follow God's counsel and not the devil's.

The priest gave her a book about a sinful woman in the gospel, which she read with genuine contrition, covering the pages with her tears. At the entry to the chapel at Chanceaux, one can read engraved on the stone, 'In this church Eve Lavallière converted and received Communion on 19 June 1917, brought back to God by Fr Chasteigner.' After returning to the sacraments, Eve insisted on abandoning the theatre as well, and seriously considered joining the Carmelite order. To prove her sincerity, she began to stop using make-up and hair dye, but her attempts to enter the order were not successful. The nuns were afraid the publicity would be too disruptive to their way of life.

She returned to Paris, sold all her wealth, and gave the money to the poor. Then she settled into a small country village called Thuillières in north-east France, where she devoted herself to prayer and joined the third order of St Francis. She also became part of a lay mission team, nursing Arab children from Tunisia.

It is possible for a person to become a saint in a short time. As if Ève was making up for lost time, and in contrast to the decades of fame and promiscuity, she quickly entered into another world of prayer and silence, of service and charity. This period, however, resulted in her contracting a fever peculiar to the North African region, and she spent the next eighteen months struggling with its symptoms. Her beautiful features were destroyed, though her large eyes still continued to shine with light. Ève offered this suffering to God in reparation for her previous sins.

Weakened by her exertions, Ève died in 1929. She was quietly buried at the base of the wall of the church in the town. Gone were the adoring audiences; only a few relatives were present. Part of a prayer she had written had indeed been realised: 'O my Redeemer, give me especially holy humility'.

FRANCIS DE SALES
(1567~1622)

A lot has happened in 500 years! A significant anniversary is fast approaching and it will be celebrated by many Christians throughout the world. In late October 1517 a young and very zealous Augustinian monk called Martin Luther nailed some ninety-five theses to the door of the cathedral in Wittenberg, Germany. Nothing more might have been heard of them if an enterprising printer had not snatched them from the door and used the new technology of the printing press to spread the word. It was the beginning of the Protestant Reformation. Thankfully we have come a long way from the polemical language and vitriol of the immediate decades and centuries afterwards. But it was not always so.

The Reformation evoked a variety of responses on the part of Catholic apologists. Some reacted defensively and with a certain amount of aggression. Others responded differently, and read the signs of the times as an occasion for conversion and repentance. One such was Francis de Sales who was born in 1567 and who later became Bishop of Geneva in Switzerland. He realised that the Church badly needed *renewal* though not *reformation*. It is the same in every age! 'Ecclesia semper renovanda est' as distinct from 'Ecclesia semper reformanda est'!

Initially Francis was destined for the world of law. His wealthy parents aspired for him to follow such a career, and the young man obliged their ambition even to the point of earning a doctorate in the subject. Internally there was a lot of tension, however. 'God does not want me to embrace the life for which my father destines me', he wrote. With the support of the then Bishop of Geneva, he studied and was ordained to the priesthood in 1593.

The Protestant cause was advanced in that part of the world. The Chablais area around the city of Geneva had become completely Calvinist and many Catholic churches and properties had been burned. However, the Catholic Duke of Savoy reconquered the area and requested the bishop to allow priests to return. This was a daunting task for there was still much hostility towards the Catholic Church. Nevertheless, Francis volunteered.

The next few years were extremely difficult. Francis travelled up and down the region, living in poverty, relying on alms, experiencing some very cold winters. On some occasions he barely escaped assassination. Above all he had to work hard at overcoming the prejudice people had against the Catholic faith. The legacy bequeathed to him was sad. Not by force, but by love and self-sacrifice, he sought to return the hearts of people to their ancient faith. Many hundreds of families were reconciled with the Church as a result of his mission at this time.

In the year 1602 Francis was made bishop of Geneva. As the city remained a Calvinist stronghold, there was simply no way that he could take possession of his See. Instead he went to the nearby town of Annecy in France. From there he administered his diocese as best he could. During this whole time, he continued to grow in reputation as a preacher and also as a compassionate and understanding bishop. Indeed, his diocese became known throughout Europe for its efficient organisation and zealous clergy as well its well-instructed laity. It was a monumental achievement for this or any age. Indeed, the very reasons for which people had been so critical of the clergy before could not be found in Francis. During his years as bishop he acquired a reputation as an ascetic who had a great love for the poor. Listening and understanding were two of his greatest traits.

One of Francis' principal achievements was working closely with the Capuchin order. Indeed, the Capuchins appreciated his cooperation so much that they made him an official associate of the Order. Tradition has it that at Evian (famous for its water today) St Francis of Assisi appeared to him and said, 'You desire martyrdom, just as I once longed for it. But, like me, you will not obtain it. You will have to become an instrument of your own martyrdom.'

One of the fruits of the Reformation was a greater awareness of the role of lay people within the Church. Francis was equally aware of the importance of the lay vocation, and in many ways anticipated the vision and documents of the Second Vatican Council. His main writing in this regard was the *Introduction to the Devout Life*, which – unusual for that time – was written especially for lay people. In the passage which is chosen by the Church for the Office of Readings for his feast, Francis offers an understanding of the different paths to God and the different vocations that lead there: 'Tell me please, my Philothea, whether it is proper for a bishop to want to lead a solitary life like a Carthusian or for married people to be no more concerned than a Capuchin about increasing their income; or for a working man to spend his whole day in church like a religious; or for a religious to be constantly exposed like a bishop to all the events and circumstances that bear on the needs of our neighbour.'

In December 1622 Francis arrived in the city of Lyons; he was in the entourage of Charles Emmanuel, Duke of Savoy, for the Duke's Christmas visit of his domain. When he arrived in the city he chose to stay not in the palace, but in the gardener's hut, and there it was on 28 December that he suffered a stroke and died. Despite the resistance of the people of Lyons, his body was taken to Annecy for interment and there he was buried in the Monastery of the Visitation. His feast day is celebrated on 24 January each year, which was the day of his burial. Francis was beatified in 1661 by Pope Alexander VII and canonised by the same Pope four years later.

Paraphrasing the words of Pope John Paul at Knock, we pray that in this very different age, and in a Europe that has largely forgotten its Christian roots, the followers of Martin Luther and Francis de Sales may be enabled to work together, 'to conquer a new continent for Christ'.

GIUSEPPE 'PINO' PUGLISI
(1937~1993)

It's sad but true: evil fascinates us. The sinister and macabre reaches into our hidden depths. Why are there so many TV series about serial killers? When lists are made of the most popular films of all time, why do they almost invariably feature violence and conflict? Is it a symptom of our fallen nature?

Despite our fascination with this dark side, however, there is also a chilling awareness of the awfulness of evil. A few years ago on a visit to the south of Italy, where one of the most notorious gangs (the 'Ndràngheta) rules, Pope Francis condemned the Mafia in no uncertain terms. Yet, a few weeks later, during a Marian procession in the town, a grotesque gesture was made. Despite the local bishop's objection, one of the floats with a huge statue of Our Lady took a detour, and passed the house of the senior 'Don' who was under house arrest at the time. Here the float bearers made the statue bow in front of the house. It was a brutal act of defiance, tragically fitting with the nature of the Mafia.

Some time ago I found myself in Palermo Cathedral in Sicily. While admiring its stunning beauty and grandeur, I noticed a small exhibition in one corner dedicated to a priest named Giuseppe Puglisi. I learned that this priest had stood up to the Mafia some twenty years earlier, and that in the end they had taken his life.

The story of Giuseppe begins in the Brancaccio area of Palermo, the capital city of Sicily, the large island to the south of Italy. His parents were simple but hardworking people, his father being a shoemaker and his mother a dressmaker. At the age of sixteen he entered the seminary and, alongside his studies, worked in various parishes. But the tentacles of the Mafia reached even into the heart of the Church. The prelate who ordained Giuseppe, Cardinal Ernesto Ruffini, saw communism as a greater threat than the Mafia, and to a large extent turned a blind eye to the power of that organisation. 'What is the Mafia?' a journalist asked him on one occasion, to which he replied, 'As far as I know, it could be a brand of detergent'. Fr Puglisi was appalled at this attitude, and decided that the Church had a duty to stand up to the monstrous evil that was in their midst.

In 1960 Fr Puglisi returned to his native Brancaccio and became the priest of the parish of San Gaetano. From the start, he tried to change his parishioners' mentality, which was conditioned by fear and passivity, and above all by the code of imposed silence called *omertà*. He encouraged them to give information about the Mafia's activities even if they could not actually give names to the police. He refused any money from Mafia sources, often obtained illegally, and would not allow the Mafia 'men of honour' to walk at the head of processions. Giuseppe also encouraged the children not to drop out of school, because being vulnerable they were likely to fall under the sway of dealers in contraband cigarettes and drugs. He refused to award contracts to Mafia-friendly firms for parish repairs.

Needless to say, all this did not endear him to the Mafia. Parishioners began to receive threatening phone calls or find their front doors torched. One evening, 15 September 1993, Fr Giuseppe was shot in front of his church by a single shot. Though doctors tried to save him, he died later that evening in the hospital. His death had been ordered by the local Mafia bosses. One of the hitmen who killed him later confessed to the crime, and revealed that the priest's last words before he shot him were, 'I've been expecting you'. The killers were later jailed.

Italy was shocked by the killing, and although Pope John Paul did not attend the funeral – he was in Tuscany at the time – he praised Fr Puglisi just over a year later when he visited the island. The Pope urged the Sicilians not to allow the priest's death to have been in vain. Soon one of Giuseppe's favourite sayings, *Se ognuno fa qualcosa, allora si può fare molto* ('If everyone does something, then we can do a lot'), was scrawled everywhere on the walls of Brancaccio. His message was taking root. Within a few years his cause was introduced in Rome, and in 2013 he was beatified in front of 50,000 people in the centre of Palermo.

There is a scene in the third of The Godfather trilogy in which the Godfather (Al Pacino) finds himself alone in a beautiful garden with a Cardinal with whom he is trying to do some legitimate business. There is a moment of grace in their conversation, when the Cardinal, sensing an opportunity, allows the years of diplomatic training to slip away and he becomes the priest again in search of a soul. The film leaves us still wondering at the end if confession was really made and absolution given, but it is a moment of real awakening. There is also another memorable moment when the cardinal takes a small stone from the well in the centre of the garden and smashes it against the side of the well. 'You see this stone?' he asks, holding the two broken pieces. 'This is what so much of Europe is like: on the outside wet, washed for centuries by the gospel; but on the inside totally dry, as if completely untouched by its values and its message.' A harsh analysis? Perhaps.

But in the midst of so much evil, there are signs of the power of grace at work too, inspired by the courage of people like Giuseppe Puglisi. 'The blood of the martyrs,' Tertullian said way back in the third century, 'is the seed of the Church.' Giuseppe Puglisi's death will not be in vain.

HENRI LACORDAIRE
(1802~1861)

People of faith received a severe battering during the years of the French Revolution, which began in 1789. The monarchy and aristocracy came to be reviled. Everything associated with the *ancien régime* was also jettisoned, including the Church. Religious orders were suppressed and churches were closed. The Church in France went into hibernation for many years. It sounds depressingly familiar, doesn't it?

Yet the Lord never abandons his Church. In every age he raises up men and women as beacons and models to inspire others whose faith is being attacked and undermined. One such example in this period was Jean-Baptiste Henri Lacordaire, who was born in 1802. By that time, local churches, especially in the countryside, were beginning to reopen, and religious life in France was starting to emerge from its hibernation. His mother saw to it that he was baptised and received some initial catechesis.

Initially, Henri showed no great inclination to serve the Church. Instead, he studied law in his hometown of Dijon. Yet the memory of his mother's lively faith continued to haunt him, and often his friends found him quietly praying in some local chapel. He admitted that he had 'a most religious heart and a very incredulous mind'. He knew deep down, however, that one day he would live a Christian life. 'I fancy I see a man', he wrote, 'groping his way blindfolded; the bandage is gradually withdrawn; he has a glimmering of the daylight, and at the moment when the handkerchief falls, he stands in the broad daylight.'

Lacordaire felt that the 'broad daylight' in which he was standing was still in need of guidance. The nation, which had sought liberty, equality and fraternity, was also prey to various other philosophies, as the revolutionary years had shown. Henri saw that the forces of atheism and rationalism were still around. His analysis of the Church at the time was equally sharp. 'What do the priests in the parishes do?' he asked. 'They maintain the knowledge of Christian truths among women, a few men, few youths. From time to time, they withdraw from the environment of error a few souls. Shut up within their sanctuary, they are incapable of defending it from the attacks from outside.'

Lacordaire decided to give up the legal profession and become a priest. In the seminary he was a bit of a maverick, and often questioned the professors in class; because of his brilliance and depth in prayer, however, he was accepted for ordination to the priesthood in 1827. His first attempts at reform were marked by turbulence. He teamed up with a fiery old priest, called Félicité Robert de Lamennais, and together they produced a newspaper called *L'Avenir*, which means 'The Future'. Its purpose was to attack the government where it sought to jeopardise the Church's growing freedom. It also attacked the Church where it seemed to be weak and accommodating. Naturally, the attacks drew the ire of many, and within a year the paper was silenced by the Church authorities. Lacordaire accepted the decision, but Lamennais refused, and ended up not only leaving the priesthood but also the Church.

Lacordaire then took a quieter and more withdrawn role. His reputation as a man of God and of outstanding intellect, however, drew many young Catholics to petition the Archbishop of Paris to allow Lacordaire to give a series of sermons during Lent in the great Cathedral of Notre Dame in that city. After some hesitation the bishop agreed, permitting Lacordaire to preach without a prepared text. This was unusual for the time, since it was normal then to use prepared material, more or less consisting of the recitation of Church doctrines and moral teachings. This format tended to produce very little creativity, and so did not touch the minds and hearts of the young.

Every Sunday in the Lenten and Easter seasons of 1835, Lacordaire preached in the cathedral, and not a seat could be found! People arrived hours before the sermon began in order to hear him. In his talks, he spoke about the nature of the Church, its prophetic teaching, and the positive effects that Catholic teaching should have on society. He always spoke with great respect for his listeners' quest for truth, yet he made no excuses for his disagreements with philosophies which denied the truth of the gospel.

Despite his popularity with the young, there were still some who were deeply suspicious of him. Loyal to the Church's older ways, they considered him a dangerous influence, and could not separate him from his former ally, Lamennais. Many of his detractors were unrelenting, and the following year, before a stunned congregation, Lacordaire announced his retirement from the pulpit.

He went to Rome to study theology further, and to pray. There he met Pope Gregory XVI as well as a few cardinals who were sympathetic and supportive. It was while he was in Rome that he saw afresh the strength of the religious orders, especially the Dominicans – the Order of Preachers – who had been suppressed in France in 1790. He spent the next ten years trying to establish the Dominicans in France, having by that stage entered the order in Rome himself. By 1849 there were several houses established throughout France.

In 1841, he resumed his conferences in Notre Dame during the seasons of Advent, Lent and Easter. People could see and hear for themselves what could happen when challenging, intelligent and creative preaching took place. One can imagine the effect of this great preacher as he spoke in eloquent tones. 'Holiness is the love of God and of men carried to a sublime extravagance', he said. 'That sublime extravagance dates from a yet higher and more unutterable folly: of a God dying upon a cross, his head crowned with thorns, his feet and hands pierced, his body bruised and mutilated.' His most famous statement, perhaps, is that concerning the priesthood: 'To live in the midst of the world without wishing its pleasures; to be a member of each family, yet belonging to none; to share all sufferings; to penetrate all secrets; to heal all wounds; to go from men to God and offer him their prayers; to return from God to men to bring pardon and hope; to have a heart of fire for charity and a heart of bronze for chastity; to teach and to pardon, console and bless always. My God, what a life! And it is yours, O priest of Jesus Christ.'

In later life, after a brief abortive attempt to enter politics and bring Catholicism into the public arena, Lacordaire retired permanently from public life to spend more time with his confrères. He took up teaching in schools in Lyon, and later Sorèze, and entered this phase of his life filled with the same enthusiasm as he had all others. He died on 20 November 1861, having spent his last few years in relative seclusion. To the end, he remained an enigma. Why, people wondered, did he retire from society when he wanted so much to change it?

He remains a prophetic voice for our changing times. When others wanted to bring about liberty and democracy without the gospel, Lacordaire was convinced of the need to be faithful to Christ in the pursuit of the same aims. Rationalism without God exalted humanity beyond its proper limits, and eventually led to each person following their own reason. There was no room for absolute truth in such a scheme. Today, we live in a different era and another country. Yet we are experiencing something of the same vacuum which Lacordaire knew so well in his beloved France. The words of Cardinal Joseph

Ratzinger, written before he became Pope Benedict XVI and published in *Salt of the Earth* in 1996, could well have been said by the great French preacher:

I find very interesting the image of the black holes, of collapsing stars. The historical hour isn't turning around, nor is this star becoming compact again, as it were, or returning to its accustomed size and luminosity. It would undoubtedly be false to expect that an historical shift should take place and that the faith will again become a large-scale mass phenomenon that dominates history.

But I continue to believe that there are also silent revolutions, that the Church is once more, so to speak, reassembling herself from the pagans, and that in this sense the experience of Jesus and of his disciples repeats itself.

In the light of recent scientific discoveries, might one think that the Pope Emeritus was anticipating some new gravitational waves of faith.

JOHN WESLEY
(1703~1791)

'Work! Work! Work! I have so much work to do today I must begin
with three hours of prayer.' Only a saint could have said that! How
often, when we get busy, do we skimp on prayer, 'saving time' in order
to catch up on our work? If John Wesley, a mighty man of prayer,
had been born a Catholic he would long since have been declared a
saint, a great saint of our Church. When I think of the mighty evan-
gelists who truly made a difference in our world, I think of St Paul, St
Columban, St Francis Xavier – and John Wesley, the great Methodist
of the eighteenth century.

How differently things might have been if John had not survived
a fire in his house in 1709, when he was very young. In later life, he
reflected that God 'had plucked him like a branch from the fire', ap-
plying to himself a verse from the Prophet Zechariah *(3:2)*. He saw in
this event the merciful hand of God entering into his life. There was
mercy too in God's choice of John and his brother Charles to be part
of the renewal of the Church in England in their own time.

By the beginning of the eighteenth century, the Church of England
had been reduced to a desperate state. The worship had become dull
and very formal, church buildings had been allowed to fall into de-
cay, the poor were neglected and the clergy had become cynical and
worldly.

The Wesley household had known no such indifference. Susanna was the mother of the house and was exacting in every way. She imparted to her eighteen children – of whom the youngest, Charles, was the great hymn writer – a sense of holiness that remained with them to the end. When the brothers went to university they formed a 'holy club' to attract those students who took their faith seriously. In the club the brothers had a purpose and a method, and so they were given a nickname: Methodists. John became the natural leader of the group.

Yet, despite their best efforts, something was still missing in their approach. They went as missionaries to Georgia in America, but their preaching proved to be ineffective. The slaveholders were antagonistic to their sermons, and the brothers saw little fruit from their labours. Their ministry was honest and dutiful, but it lacked any real impact. Returning to England, they both experienced a conversion when they took part in a prayer meeting in a Moravian chapel in May 1738. 'I felt my heart strangely warmed,' John was later to recount, 'I felt I did trust in Christ, Christ alone for salvation and an assurance was given me that he had taken away my sins, even mine, and saved me from the law of sin and death.'

Right to the end John saw himself as an Anglican, with Methodism as a branch within the wider Church. But, from his new perspective, he saw the good folk of England around him as 'sheep without a shepherd', and he wanted so much to bring them to know the mercy and love of God. 'I look upon the world as my parish,' he said, 'I judge it meet and my bounden duty to declare unto all who are willing to hear the glad tidings of salvation. This is the work which I know God has called me to.'

A year after his initial conversion, in 1739, John experienced a further conversion. It happened when the great English preacher, George Whitefield, invited him to an open-air service. The location took John completely by surprise. 'I should have thought the saving of souls almost a sin if it had not been done in a church', he later wrote. This simple event opened up new possibilities for John, and was the beginning of the great eighteenth-century evangelical revival.

Renewal and conversion generally provoke two contradictory reactions: enthusiasm and resistance. Jesus, we know, had his scribes and pharisees as well as his followers. While many were attracted to the 'new faith' John and his brother were preaching, there were many others in the established Church who closed their hearts and their pulpits to them. John in particular was forced to become 'God's horseman', travelling up and down the length and breadth of England – and beyond – preaching wherever people gathered: in the fields, at crossroads, near the inns. In all, it is reckoned that he preached more than 40,000 sermons, often speaking several times a day.

Despite his own energy and enthusiasm, however, John knew that he could not reach the vast population on his own. In time, Wesley started to evaluate and approve men who were not ordained by the Anglican Church to preach and do pastoral work. This expansion of lay preachers proved to be one of the main reasons for the growth of Methodism in the land. It is a feature which remains to this day.

While, of course, there were – and are – differences between Wesley's creed and Catholicism, the great preacher did not dismiss the older Church in the vehement way that many others did at that time. In his *Letter to a Roman Catholic*, written from Dublin in July 1749 after sectarian riots there, he was at pains to find the common ground between the two faiths; above all he acknowledged the Christian roots and strengths of the Church of Rome.

Not surprisingly, the years of preaching and travelling took their toll on John. He died on 2 March 1791. As he lay dying, with his friends gathered round him, he grasped their hands, saying repeatedly, 'Farewell, farewell'. At the end, he said, 'The best of all is, God is with us'.

John Wesley died completely poor, having given away everything during his life. But he left behind him 135,000 members and 541 itinerant preachers, people who had truly been 'born again'. At this time in our own land, Catholics can learn much from a man who thought outside the box, one who effectively engaged the laity in his mission, a holy man of God who needed to pray three hours a day before he ventured out the door!

JULIAN OF NORWICH
(c.1342~c.1416)

One of the most beautiful sentences in any language was written some six centuries ago by this woman, about whom we still know relatively little. More about that later.

The late fourteenth century was a time of terrible upheaval. With the Black Death, the Hundred Years War and the crisis of Church authority occasioned by the long papal schism – when for almost seventy years the French-born Popes held the papal court at Avignon in France instead of Rome – Europe as a whole was burdened by an atmosphere of anxiety, and many people had a deep concern about the prospects of personal salvation. Added to this were doubts about the efficacy of the Church and its prescribed channels of spirituality. This led in turn to the development of new spiritualities developed by lay people outside of the conventional religious orders. There was a real flowering of non-monastic mysticism.

England in particular produced a large number of mystical classics at this time, written often by lay people for other laity as they sought a more intimate relationship with God. *The Cloud of Unknowing* was one such classic that had wide circulation. *Revelations of Divine Love* by Julian of Norwich was another widely read work that remains influential even in our own time. Julian herself was an anchoress.

In the late Middle Ages, it was not unknown for men to become anchorites and women to become anchoresses. It was a severe form of religious life where people became recluses within an enclosure. The enclosure was sometimes attached to a larger religious house which provided for all their material needs. Their vocation then was to devote themselves to prayer and fasting. It demanded a commitment for life, and in order to stress the finality of the undertaking the burial service was read at their consecration, signifying that the person enclosed was dead to the world and that the enclosure corresponded to a grave. The overall purpose of the enclosure was to allow those called to commit themselves without distraction to a life of prayer and contemplation.

In the year 1373, Julian of Norwich was about thirty when she began to have a series of 'revelations'. When she was younger she had prayed for three graces: recollection of Christ's passion, bodily sickness, and the 'three wounds' of contrition, compassion and longing for God. One of her prayers was answered when she fell so seriously ill that she was given the last rites of the Church. She was indeed expected to die. Then on the seventh day the crisis passed and she had a series of visions, fifteen in all, in which she was led to contemplate the passion of Christ.

She described herself as a 'simple creature unlettered' when she received these visions, but the book to which she gave birth was the fruit of twenty years of prayer and reflection on those moments of intense intimacy with the Lord. Initially she wrote a short version of the *Shewings*, as she sometimes called them, but a longer version appeared when she had time – over many years – to meditate on the experiences.

Above all else the *Revelations of Divine Love* is a tender meditation on God's eternal and all-embracing love, as expressed for us in the passion of Jesus. The book contains some beautiful images and ideas. In her first revelation she sees Christ's crown of thorns. She writes about 'the red blood running down from under the crown, hot and flowing, freely and copiously like a stream', an image she accepts as 'hideous and fearful' but which she also proclaims as 'sweet and lovely'. This combination of adjectives is typical of Julian's work and, indeed, of her overall optimistic attitude to life and faith. For her, the cross is not a source of terror and anguish but of consolation, a sign of Christ's 'friendliness and courtesy'. God pays her the honour of a king who condescends to familiarity with a servant. Physically she sees a bleeding head. Spiritually she sees into the depths of God's love and goodness.

Elsewhere she describes seeing God holding a tiny thing in his hand, like a small brown nut, which to her eyes appeared so fragile and insignificant. She came to understand that this was the entire created universe. She came to see that physically it is nothing, but spiritually its value is measured in terms of God's love and the price Christ has paid for it in his blood. Then she was told, 'God made it, God loves it, God keeps it'. For all its weakness and sin, God suffered for this world, and in the end God's suffering is turned to joy. For our Creator is also our Lover, working good through all manner of things. We are 'soul and body, clad and enclosed in the goodness of God'.

Although she lived in a time of turmoil, her own simple theology was optimistic. Popular opinion, magnified by current events like the Black Death and other catastrophes, assumed that God was in some way punishing the wicked. In response, Julian suggested a more merciful vision. At one point she had been greatly troubled by the fate of those who had never heard the gospel, and wondered about their salvation. She never received a direct answer to her question, except to be told that whatever God does is done in love and therefore will turn out for the best in the end. It is in that spirit that she was inspired to write that powerful sentence, 'And all shall be well, and all shall be well, and all manner of things shall be well'. That is the beautiful and reassuring sentence to which I referred at the start of this chapter.

For Julian, the God who created us out of love and who redeemed us by suffering, also sustains us and wishes to be united with us at the end. This love, and not sin, fundamentally determines our existence. Evil has no independent status; whatever we may suffer God has already suffered. 'The worst', she noted, 'has already happened and been repaired'.

Julian died about the year 1416 and, although she is not a canonised saint of the Church, she is honoured on 13 May each year, particularly in the East Anglia region of England. 'And all shall be well' – what a wonderful thought to carry with us every day!

KATERI TEKAKWITHA
(1656~1680)

Kateri Tekakwitha: it is a mouthful, isn't it? The first time I came across this beautiful name was about twenty years ago. A little girl in my confirmation class had chosen the name. Among all the Patricks and Bernadettes, Michaels and Brieges, she had picked Kateri, and I had to admit I had never heard of her. Initially I was a little suspicious. Could it be the name of a soap actress, or a Hollywood film star, or a drummer in a girl band, and not the name of a saint, as I had suggested would be most appropriate? However, I was soon put right by the little girl who had chosen so thoughtfully this name from a far-off country.

In 1656, near the Mohawk river in what is now upstate New York, a girl was born to a Mohawk father and an Algonquin mother. The girl's name was Tekakwitha, which some people have translated as 'putting things right'. Her mother, who had become a Christian through the evangelisation of the Jesuits, had been captured by the Mohawks during the conquest of the Algonquin tribe. In her adopted tribe, she had to keep her faith quiet, but even so she sometimes prayed in secret with another Christian woman.

When she was four, Tekakwitha's entire family contracted smallpox; only the little girl survived. She was taken care of by Anastasia, her mother's Christian friend. Sadly, however, as a result of the disease,

Tekakwitha herself was left with a pocked face, poor eyesight and weakened legs. Her name, according to an alternative translation, means, 'the one who walks groping for the way'. These disfigurements isolated her from the other Mohawk women, but in some way they also prepared her for the later joy of finding Christ and discovering that he loved her unconditionally. Some members of her tribe said that the Creator had left her in darkness for her to see his light.

Tekakwitha was already becoming a Christian by desire during her later childhood and teenage years. A treaty between the French and the Iroquois tribe allowed some Jesuits to come to her village and preach. Her uncle did not like the Blackrobes, as the Jesuits were called, and their strange new religion, but he nevertheless tolerated the missionaries' presence. Kateri, remembering her mother's whispered prayers, was fascinated by the stories she heard about Jesus and wanted to learn more. One of the priests, Fr Jacques de Lamberville, persuaded her uncle to allow Tekakwitha to attend the religion classes, and the following Easter, at the age of twenty, she was baptised. She took the name Kateri, which was a Mohawk version of Catherine. This step, however, and her new-found joy and enthusiasm did not endear her to the other members of her tribe, and she was often scorned and persecuted by them. For instance, her family refused her food on Sundays because she would not work on that day. Sometimes children would taunt her and throw stones at her.

Eventually, a priest arranged that she should escape northwards to where she could live with other Christians. She made her way to the area around the great St Lawrence river, and in that region, near modern-day Montreal, she spent her time helping the old and the sick, and teaching the children. She made her First Holy Communion on Christmas day 1677. Although not formally educated and unable to read or write, Kateri led a life of prayer and penance. Her favourite devotion was to make crosses out of sticks and place them throughout the woods where she lived. These served as reminders to passers-by to spend a moment in prayer. She herself would often spend hours before the Blessed Sacrament, kneeling in the cold chapel by herself. When the winter season took many of the villagers away on hunting expeditions, she would be left to erect her own little chapel in the woods by carving a cross on a tree and spending time there in prayer.

Sometimes it can take decades for God to make a man or woman into a saint: our fallen nature in its obstinacy is often like Jacob wrestling with God. At other times, however, God can make a saint very quickly, as if to show us how easy it is for him to act. Such was the case with Kateri. Within a very short time, she came to be filled with God's presence and love. On one occasion, a priest asked the people why they gathered around her in church. They told him that they felt particularly close to God when Kateri prayed: her face changed and she became full of peace and beauty, as if she were looking at the face of God himself.

Today, physical beauty is so highly prized that those less favoured by nature or marred by illness can have difficulty in believing that they are indeed beautiful or that anyone could love them. In spite of her own weak body and marked face, Kateri radiated a real inner beauty to everyone with whom she came into contact. Many of us will remember that same beauty in the aged face of Mother Teresa when she was alive. Others may recall too the serene peace on the face of Br Roger Schutz, the founder of the Taizé community in France who, though ninety years of age at his death in 2005, radiated a beauty and tranquillity beyond words.

According to legends at the time, Kateri's scars vanished at the time of her death, revealing a woman of immense beauty. It was claimed too that on the day of her funeral many of the sick who attended were healed. The poor health which plagued her throughout her life had led to an early death at the age of twenty-four. Her last words were,

'Jesus, I love you'. Kateri has sometimes been called 'The Lily of the Mohawks'. Like the flower after which she was named, her life was short and beautiful.

Pope John Paul II beatified Kateri on 22 June 1980, and on 19 December 2011 Pope Benedict XVI canonised her. She was the first native American to be so honoured. Her feast day is celebrated on 14 July.

KATHARINE DREXEL
(1858~1955)

'How hard it is for a rich man to enter the Kingdom of Heaven', Jesus said. The apostles, we are told, were astounded by these words of the Master. 'In that case,' they wondered, 'who can be saved?'

God bless the apostles, but they were certainly thinking within a time-honoured framework, which said that wealth was a sign of God's blessing. Today, many people in parts of the developed world subscribe to what is called 'the prosperity gospel'. Jesus was inviting his disciples to see and think differently. While they were impressed by those who put a lot of money into the treasury, Jesus picked out a little old woman who put in a tiny coin; he told them that she had put in more than all the others, because she had given her all.

Many years ago I participated in a wonderful retreat for priests in the city of Rome, marking the start of the decade of evangelisation inaugurated by Pope John Paul. About 7,500 priests from all over the world attended and heard the call to spread the good news. It was marvellous to see hundreds of men from developing countries taking part, but their attendance was only made possible by the generosity of one man, Piet Derksen, a sort of Dutch Billy Butlin or Fred Pontin. He used the profits from his holiday camps to promote good causes, including the work of Catholic evangelisation.

The saint we recall in this chapter fits into a similar category as

Piet. In 1858 Francis and Hannah Drexel were proud parents of a second daughter, Katharine, but sadly, just one month after the birth, Hannah passed away. Her father, who was a well-known and prosperous banker, married again a few years later and both parents instilled in their children the idea that wealth was meant to be shared with others, especially the poor. Indeed, Katharine's father even had one servant whose job was solely to look after the poor who came to the door of their house in Philadelphia in the United States – and there were plenty of visitors!

Katharine's family background and, later, her schooling with the Sisters of the Sacred Heart, prepared her well for the vocation which lay ahead. Her stepmother allowed her and her sisters to run a Sunday school for the children of her father's employees.

As she grew into a young woman, Katharine spent her time and money doing good in obedience to a personal revelation that she felt had come from Our Lady: 'Freely you have received; freely give'. The cause which most interested her was the plight of the Native Americans and African Americans, whose living and educational situations were often deplorable. Before starting her own order, she gave huge sums of money to anyone who was able to establish schools for these disadvantaged people. 'Use money, tainted as it is, to win you friends', Jesus had said. Katherine was certainly obedient to that word.

A key moment in the life of Katharine Drexel was a trip to Rome in 1887, as part of a tour of Europe. The family were privileged to receive an audience with the Pope, Leo XIII. In a moment of conversation, Katherine pleaded with the Pope to send more missionaries to Wyoming for her friend, Bishop James O'Connor. The Pope replied, 'Why don't *you* become a missionary?'

The question ended her doubts about entering religious life, and Katharine, with the full approval of her family, began to use the money at her disposal to found a motherhouse for the young women who were around her and who were eager to pursue the vision Katharine had instilled in them. The year was 1891. Initially Katharine's order was called the Sisters of the Blessed Sacrament for Indians and Coloured People, which illustrated her dual love for the Eucharist and her deep concern for the poorest of the poor in American society at that time. Today it is simply known as the Sisters of the Blessed Sacrament.

Her work was to provide education and training for those who came from the disenfranchised peoples of the United States. The first mission school for Native Americans opened in Santa Fe, New Mexico. Other schools quickly followed under her direction, for Native Americans west of the river Mississippi and for the African Americans in the southern part of the United States. Indeed, one college, Xavier University in New Orleans, became the first predominantly black Catholic institution in the States.

In 1935 Katharine suffered a severe heart attack, but lived on to the ripe age of ninety-seven in prayerful retirement, until her death on 3 March 1955. At the time of her death there were more than 500 sisters in the Order, teaching in sixty-three schools and institutes across the States.

Katharine was beatified by Pope John Paul on 20 November 1988, and canonised by the same Pope on 1 October 2000, becoming only the second native-born American saint, after Elizabeth Seton.

MARIA SOLEDAD
(1826~1887)

Maggie died almost fifty years ago. I used to visit her in her small cramped flat on the fourth floor of a crowded apartment block. Life had not been kind to her: she had no family, no apparent relatives, no friends. She had had no career, just bits of work from time to time to make ends meet; and old age was creeping up fast. There was a sadness about her face, even though she tried to be pleasant when I called.

One day, after many months of visiting her from the seminary, there was no answer to my knock. Thinking she might be out, I left and vowed to call the next day – and the next. Eventually I called the police – there was no one else to do so – and we found that Maggie had died several days earlier. The flies had begun to gather. Some days later the local council helped to bury her and I persuaded some friends from the seminary to help me carry the coffin as we lowered her body on a wet and windy day. No one deserves to leave this earth in this way.

My story here reminds me of a woman who knew many of the Maggies of the world. That was her ministry. Indeed, she became a mother to the shut-ins of her time and those who had no one to visit them. Antonia Manuela Torres was born in Madrid in Spain in 1826, the daughter of a small businessman. As she grew into adulthood, she became inspired by the example and words of a priest called Miguel Martinez y Sanz who worked in one of the slums of the great city. He was quite an extraordinary man in his own right.

As in so many other cities throughout the world, labourers from the farms were coming to Madrid looking for work and basic housing to provide for their needs. Antonia had received spiritual direction from Fr Miguel and he had suggested that there was need for an order in the Church that would visit the abandoned sick, many of whom were poor and could not afford even elementary health care.

At the age of twenty-one Antonia began visiting the homes of both rich and poor. At first she was revolted by some of the diseases she encountered and by the sight of corpses, but she overcame her fears by trying to see Christ in each person. I am reminded of St Teresa of Calcutta's dictum about 'recognising Christ in the distressing disguise of the poor'. As Antonia's work progressed and others began to join in her enterprise, a new order was formed in the Church. On August 15 1851, the 24-year-old Antonia and six others took the three religious vows of poverty, chastity and obedience, and received the habit of the new congregation. They also took on new names, and Antonia became Sr Maria Soledad. A few years later, she was appointed superior of the community.

The fledgling community was not without its difficulties; sometimes there was scarcely enough food even for the sisters. Yet Maria participated in all the ordinary work that needed to be done every day: washing clothes at the river, gathering firewood and cooking. 'Do not be so anxious about a house on earth', she told her sisters, 'when we have such a beautiful one in heaven'. On another occasion she encouraged them to be faithful to their vision: 'We are poor but charity compels us. We must share what God gives us among the poor.'

Sr Maria had the joy of seeing her little congregation grow, and in time it was given full papal approval by Pope Pius IX in 1876. But the years of work had taken their toll and Maria succumbed to pneumonia at the age of sixty. In 1887 she died at the original motherhouse of the order. Beatification and canonisation followed in in 1950 and 1970 respectively. At the time of her death there were forty-six houses of the Servants of Mary in Europe and South America.

Is there a Maggie in your street who could be visited? Is there someone who could be invited to an upcoming parish function? Is there someone who lives alone you could offer to take to Mass? Could you drop in an apple tart to that man at the end of the street who lives alone?

I have the privilege each month as a priest of visiting many a Maggie and Tom and Séamus and Máire. The week of the First Friday is a special week in the lives of many priests and Ministers of the Eucharist, especially as they try to get round their elderly and housebound parishioners. The visit is often brief, with many calls to be made in the morning or afternoon. Yet the visit is welcomed – those few brief moments when Christ in the Eucharist is given to someone who was faithful to Mass and now cannot get out to church.

I hope I never again have to bury anyone on a wet day with only a few strangers to lower the coffin.

MARIA VON TRAPP
(1905~1987)

Readers of a certain vintage may already be humming a certain tune once they have seen the name of Maria von Trapp! *The Sound of Music* was one of the great hits of the last century. Austrians, it is reported, do not like the perceived saccharine view of their country as portrayed, but the film starring Julie Andrews and Christopher Plummer had many fans and is still popular today in TV re-runs at Christmastime and other holiday periods. The real story of Maria von Trapp is somewhat different from the one we know, however. Yes, she certainly did enter a convent and spend some time there, but a lot happened before then and her subsequent involvement with Captain von Trapp and his several children.

Maria was born and raised a Catholic. Her mother died when she was only two, and her father placed her into the care of an elderly cousin who tried to teach her some prayers and read her Bible stories. Things changed when she reached the age of nine. Her father died, and her uncle became her legal guardian. He was a fierce advocate of the new National Socialist Party – the Nazis – and had no time for religion or religious symbolism. 'At the mere mention of the word he would burst into laughter', Maria remembered.

Unfortunately, Maria began to imbibe this spirit too, and so began to think of herself as an atheist. By the time she was a young adult she had left her uncle and began to share digs with a friend. After a short period working in a hotel, she enrolled to be a teacher. Some of the Catholic girls in her class went to Mass every day, and Maria made fun of them: 'the holy water girls', she called them. She had no need of God, and filled her own spiritual void with music which had always been so important for her.

Palm Sunday 1924 was to be a pivotal moment in her life. On that day she was passing a church and, thinking that there would be a performance of Bach's *St Matthew Passion* on, she went inside. She loved music, whatever the source. Instead of Bach, however, she found herself at a Lenten lecture given by a famous Jesuit priest. Maria sat down and listened. 'I had heard from my uncle that all these Bible stories were just legends and inventions without a word of truth in them,' she later remarked, 'but the way this man talked just swept me off my feet. I was completely overwhelmed. At the end I just had to go and talk to him.'

'Do you really believe all this?' she asked the priest. He invited her back a couple of days later when he would have more time to talk. Maria duly returned, and for over two hours she threw at him all the arguments and accusations which she had heard and indeed nursed in her short life. The priest, she remembered, listened a lot more than he talked. It was a lesson in good evangelisation. As St Peter wrote in his first letter, 'If anyone asks you for the reason for the hope that you have, give it with courtesy and respect' *(1 P.3:15)*.

'As I looked back on those few hours,' Maria continued, 'I realised what happened in my soul. This priest was not only a famous theologian, a great preacher both in Germany and many English-speaking countries, but he was also a humble man who loved his Lord and Saviour. When I had finished throwing everything at him, he looked at me and began to tell me how Jesus Christ had lived, and that he had been crucified and died for me. He said it so simply that I was completely disarmed. And then he said, "Are you sorry for what has happened?" With tears streaming down my face I simply replied, "Yes, Father".'

Maria had come home. Because she was already a baptised Catholic the priest simply gave her absolution. 'God will simply eradicate your sins,' he said to her. 'Your soul will look like the soul of a newly baptised child.'

That encounter changed the direction of her life. In due course Maria graduated, and as a treat following her exams she and a few other girls went hiking in the mountains. Again this was a moment when God seemed to touch her. Overwhelmed one evening by a beautiful sunset, she opened her arms in sheer gratitude to God and asked, 'What can I give back to you?' She felt she knew the answer. Immediately on her return, she went to Salzburg and asked for directions to the strictest convent in the town. She found the Benedictine abbey of Nonnberg, rang the bell and asked the nuns for permission to stay.

Maria did her best to fit into the life, but somehow it was not for her. After two years, the wise Mother Superior recognised this, and sent her as a temporary tutor to the von Trapp family, where she was to care in a special way for one of the children who was recovering from a fever. Very soon Maria took over as governess for all the children. And then – after initial difficulties – romance began to blossom, and she married Georg von Trapp on 26 November 1927.

Meanwhile, the Nazi shrub which had been growing when Maria was a young woman had now become a massive tree. Hitler annexed Austria as part of the Third Reich in 1938, and Captain von Trapp – as the film correctly portrays – was obliged to report for naval duty. He knew he could not do this in conscience, and so with his young family – and Maria pregnant with their third child – they walked across the Alps into Italy, and eventually managed to get to the United States. There, the hills of Vermont reminded them of their homeland. Maria would never return to her beloved Austria, but she knew that she had come home long before that.

MONICA OF HIPPO
(c.331~387)

One of my favourite saints and, indeed, one whom I most often mention these days is Monica. Her feast day is on 27 August, the day before the feast day of her son, the great St Augustine, probably one of the three greatest minds in the history of the Church. I find myself mentioning Monica often in sermons, especially at funerals, and also when talking to parents whose sons or daughters no longer walk with Christ, or at least with the Church, in the faith that their parents followed.

Let us look at who this extraordinary woman was before we try to glean some lessons from her life. We know little of her childhood, except that she was born in North Africa in the year 331. She was married early in life to a man name Patritius, who held an official position in Tagaste. He was not a Christian, although his practice of his pagan religion was only nominal. Sadly, his temper was violent, and he appears to have had some wayward habits. It is even said that he beat his wife. Consequently, Monica's married life was far from being a happy one, more especially as Patritius's mother seems to have been very similar in temperament. There was, of course, a gulf between husband and wife: her alms, deeds and her habits of prayer annoyed him, but somehow he always held her in a sort of reverence.

Monica was not the only matron of Tagaste whose married life was unhappy but, by her own gentleness and patience, she was able to exercise a real apostolate amongst the wives and mothers of her native town. They knew that she suffered as they did, and her words and example had a positive effect. In due time, she won the favour of her mother-in-law by the mildness of her manner and by her patience in the midst of her difficult marriage.

Three children were born of this marriage: Augustine the eldest, Navigius the second, and a daughter, Perpetua. Monica had been unable to secure baptism for her children, and her grief was great when Augustine fell ill. In her distress, she begged Patritius to allow him to be baptised; he agreed, but on the boy's recovery, withdrew his consent.

All Monica's anxiety now centred on Augustine. Like his father before him, he too was wayward and lazy. He was sent to Madaura to school, and Monica seems to have literally wrestled with God for the soul of her son. A great consolation was given her, however, in compensation for all that she was to experience through Augustine: Patritius became a Christian.

Meanwhile, Augustine had been sent to Carthage to pursue his studies, and there he fell into serious sin. Patritius died very shortly after his reception into the Church, and Monica resolved not to marry again. At Carthage, Augustine had become a follower of the Manichean sect and when, on his return home, he aired certain heretical propositions, Monica drove him away from her table. Later she had a strange vision which urged her to take him back. Augustine, perhaps frustrated by the presence of his nagging mother, went off secretly to Milan. However, she followed him there.

It was at this time that she went to see Bishop Ambrose of Milan whom she knew Augustine liked to listen to from time to time. Initially Ambrose did not appear to have much time for her, but she persisted and the story goes that he turned around to her and consoled her with the now famous words, 'The child of those tears shall never perish'. She ultimately had the joy of seeing Augustine yield, after seventeen years of resistance. The story of his conversion – told in *The Confessions*, one of the classics of Christian literature – is a beautiful page in the annals of the saints. The voice of a child in a nearby garden – the invitation to 'take up and read' – and Augustine's obedience to the word of scripture which he read are all graphic testimony to the gentle power of God and the mercy with which he exercises it.

Mother and son spent six months of true peace at Cassiacum, after which time Augustine was baptised in the Church of St John the Baptist, in Milan. Africa called to them, however, and they set out on their journey, stopping at Civitavecchia and at Ostia. Monica died here in 387 and the finest pages of Augustine's *Confessions* were penned as the result of the emotion he experienced then. In these pages, Augustine recounts how he and his brother were discussing where they might bury Monica when she died. She overheard their whispers and chided them somewhat for their concerns, with words which have come down to us through the centuries and which have appeared on millions of memorial cards: 'All I ask is that you remember me at the altar of God'. These are words I often quote at the end of a funeral sermon, knowing that the saintly parishioners I bury would also want their children and grandchildren to remember them in this way above all else.

Monica was buried at Ostia, and at first she seems to have been almost forgotten, though her body was removed during the sixth century to a hidden crypt in the church of St Aureus. About the thirteenth century, however, the cult of St Monica began to spread, and a feast in her honour is kept on 4 May.

In 1430, Pope Martin V ordered the relics of St Monica to be brought to Rome. Many miracles occurred on the way, and devotion to St Monica was definitely established. Later, the Archbishop of Rouen, Cardinal d'Estouteville, built a church in Rome in honour of St Augustine, and deposited the relics in a chapel to the left of the high altar.

Some years ago, I came across a prayer invoking the intercession of Monica for those who may have strayed from their childhood faith. I offer it to you now:

Eternal and merciful Father,
I give you thanks for the gift of your divine Son,
who suffered, died and rose for all people.
I thank you also for my Catholic faith,
and ask your help that I may grow in fidelity by prayer,
by works of charity and penance, by reflecting on your word,
and by regular participation in the sacraments of
Penance and the Holy Eucharist.
You gave St Monica a spirit of selfless love,
manifest in her constant prayer for the
conversion of her son, Augustine.
Inspired by boundless confidence in your power to move hearts,
and by the success of her prayer,
I ask the grace to imitate her constancy
in prayer for (name a person here)
who no longer shares in the intimate life of the Catholic family.
Grant through my prayer and witness,
that he/she may be open to the promptings of your Holy Spirit
to return to loving union with your people.
Grant also that my prayer be ever hopeful
and that I may never judge another,
for you alone can read hearts.
I ask this through Christ our Lord, Amen.

NIELS STENSEN
(1638~1686)

'Either that host is nothing but a piece of bread, and those who are showing it such honour are bewitched, or else it really is the body of Jesus Christ, and in that case why do I not venerate it as well?' This thought – this 'either/or' question – grabbed hold of the mind of Niels Stensen, a seventeenth-century Danish scientist, while he was attending a Corpus Christi procession in the city of Livorno in Italy. The year was 1666. The reasoning was typical of the man, and the question would not let him go until he became a Catholic the following year. In time, he became a priest and an outstanding bishop, and his exemplary life eventually led to his beatification by Pope John Paul II in 1988.

The story of Niels Stensen begins in January 1638 in Copenhagen, where a son was born to Sten Pedersen and Anne Nielsdatter. The parents were Lutherans, and entering the ministry was something that ran in the family: two of Niels's uncles were Lutheran pastors. From an early age it was obvious that the young Niels was very intelligent, and he began to specialise in the area of medicine, and particularly in the new science of anatomy. There is a fallacy prevalent today, held by many, which puts science and religion at opposite poles, as if they are always at loggerheads. For some, to be a believer suggests leaving reason outside the door, while faith is often seen as blind and unthinking. Niels Stensen pursued both, and saw no contradiction. For him it was not a question of 'either/or' but 'both/and'.

Stensen always acknowledged that, as a scientist, he was subject to a law that was good and in every respect divine. 'One sins against the majesty of God,' he wrote, 'if one refuses to look at nature's own work, and if one is content with merely reading what someone else has written about it.' He was never inclined to see anything contradictory between a scientific and a Christian attitude towards the reality we experience with our senses. 'Give me grace, O God,' he wrote on one occasion, 'to keep myself free from all sin, and especially from a rash and insufficiently thought-out judgement or opinion on things.'

As a young man, Niels spent several years both in Amsterdam University and the ancient university town of Leiden, also in Holland, from where he received a doctorate in medicine in the year 1663. At the end of his Dutch period, he travelled on to Paris. By this time Niels was acquiring a European reputation as an anatomist. One journal wrote, 'The Danish scholar is in Paris at present, and daily carries out dissections in the presence of many who are eager for knowledge.' His most beautiful writings came when he discovered new organs and glands in the bodies of both animals and human beings.

It was in Paris that his work on the human brain gained most fame. Specialists agree that it provided the basis for research over the following 200 years. His starting point was typical and commonplace: 'We shall seek the truth by raising objections against it, and we shall not allow ourselves to rest until we reach it, confirmed by manifest proof.'

Niels brought this same relentless logic to his pursuit of truth in the area of religion. As we have seen, it was his attendance at the Corpus Christi procession in 1666 which moved him to consider Catholicism. In a letter to a friend, he wrote that he 'employed every conceivable opportunity to seek the truth, convinced that God would enlighten my mind with his light, so that I could come to a position where I could acknowledge the truth that I sought with a sincere heart.' He then went on: 'I was not satisfied by discussing these questions with learned men, of whom no one can deny that many are to be found among Catholics, but I wanted to obtain information on the original text of Holy Scripture and on ancient authors. Thus on many occasions I repaired to a well-known library, and there in tranquillity and peace I consulted many ancient Greek and Hebrew manuscripts, so as not to rely only on the Latin text without examining things further and comparing it with the original texts in the other two languages.'

This examination was carried out with the same precision and critical spirit as any of Stensen's scientific investigations. After he had read and verified, examined and compared, he wrote, 'I could not escape feeling deeply convinced of the truth of what the Catholics really acknowledge'. Even after becoming a Catholic, Niels continued his work as a scientist, but within a few years he felt drawn to offer himself for the priesthood. In the year 1675, at the age of thirty-seven, he was ordained a priest. It was Holy Saturday and he celebrated his first Mass in the Church of the Most Holy Annunciation in Florence on Easter Sunday.

It was not an easy time to be a Catholic in most northern European countries. Most of his kinsmen had converted to Lutheranism since the Reformation, and Catholics were few in number. Pope Innocent XI decided to send Niels as bishop, first of all to Hanover, and then to Münster, where he was appointed Vicar Apostolic for the North. His living conditions were far from pleasant, but during his whole life as a priest, and later as a bishop, he never wanted comfort for himself. He gave away virtually everything he had and lived very frugally, in marked contrast with some of the prince bishops of that era. One duke tried to present him with a coach and six horses, in keeping with his status. He replied, 'Like St Nicholas, I would rather have two small donkeys.'

Niels laboured almost a decade in the northern mission territories and, as a vibrant preacher, was instrumental in bringing many back to the faith. After only ten years in the apostolate he died, in the year 1686, at the age of forty-eight. His body was returned to Florence, where he was buried in the Basilica of St Lawrence.

The Eucharist had been instrumental in his conversion. It was also an instrument in his sanctification of others and in his zeal for souls. 'There is only one human response to the self-giving love which shows itself on the cross and lives in the Church as the true bread of humanity', he wrote. 'The more we discover and say "yes" to this love, the less do we remain as merely ourselves. The love of Christ urges us on.' Pope John Paul II beatified Niels on 23 October 1988 with these words: 'Blessed son of the Danish land! You enliven the choir of those great people who have preceded you on the way to holiness. With them you cry: He who is mighty has done great things for me.'

Niels Stensen – the man who answered the 'either/or' question – invites us to do the same.

PATRICK
(c.387~c.461)

I am writing these words on a wet and windy October evening, shortly after my appointment as parish priest to the parish of Downpatrick, where St Patrick is buried. In the few weeks since arriving in this seed-bed of Irish faith, I have become ever more conscious of the power of this young man who, with incredible faith and courage, helped to bring a whole nation to faith. The power of one: it has always been a reality, I suppose. Think of the influence of St Paul and the number of people who came to know Christ through his witness. Or, more recently, think of young Malala Yousafzai, the youngest winner of the Nobel Peace Prize, who defied the Taliban's oppressive regime and survived an assassination attempt on her life. What an inspiration she has become, a witness to courage and truth. The power of one!

You all know the story of Patrick, either in his own sober version as told in the *Confession* or in its later versions as elaborated by legends and myths. St Patrick is one of the best-known saints in the Church calendar – the Irish diaspora has ensured that he is remembered everywhere from New York to Hong Kong – but his very popularity has also ensured that we often don't know who Patrick really was. We get caught up in the myth rather than the reality, and lose sight of the real message our national apostle has to offer. Green beer and traffic lines are all very well, but Patrick advocated something more radical than that 1,600 years ago.

Sometimes we are tempted to reject the path to sanctity, imagining that God has not dealt us a very good hand. At times like that, we need only look to Patrick's example. Remember his introduction to Ireland was involuntary. At the age of sixteen he was captured by Irish pirates and taken to our shores. He had known a somewhat comfortable life as the son of a Roman official, and now he was made to look after pigs and sheep in the cold and damp. 'I was chastened exceedingly', he wrote in the *Confession*. 'I was humbled every day in hunger and nakedness.'

In that same *Confession* we are told that he prayed 100 times a day, and again at night. It may be that, like many other young people before and since, he had not thought much about his faith until now. Finding himself in a desperate situation, however, must have turned his mind and heart to the One who could strengthen him. The prayers of his youth, no doubt, came flooding back, and he clung to them for the courage and hope they inspired. With the help of these prayers and long hours of reflection, the cold and hungry shepherd came to know Christ and to place all his trust in him. In his short writings, it is striking how often Patrick refers to Christ as a living person and a close friend.

At the same time, throughout his captivity, Patrick clung to the hope of escaping, and after six years he found an opportunity. Following a long journey of about 200 miles, he eventually found a boat which took him back to a tearful reunion with his family and friends. But Patrick was no longer the carefree adolescent of before. His faith had been forged in fire and had become strong. Waiting now for a new sense of purpose, and a new direction in life, he knew he was different.

He didn't have long to wait. As he recounts it in his *Confession*, Patrick heard the 'voice of the Irish' bidding him come and 'walk once more among us'. The young man was convinced that he had a mission from God, but instead of rushing headlong into it, he spent the next period of his life – some say twelve, some even twenty years – preparing himself for this mighty task. He studied at two great French centres of learning and spirituality – Lérins and Auxerre – where he received the necessary spiritual training and learned the practical skills of building churches which he believed he needed for his mission. In 432, he returned to Ireland as a bishop. Tradition has it that he landed at Saul on Strangford Lough, which is near to his final burial place and just a few miles from the town where I now minister.

The next thirty years were to be full of activity and fervour, some of them distorted since by legends. What cannot be denied is that Patrick consolidated the faith which others had sown in the land. He baptised thousands of people and ordained hundreds of priests to carry on the work of evangelisation. He established Armagh as the Primatial See of Ireland. He also laid down the foundations for a network of churches and monasteries throughout the land. Thousands of young men and women, many being the sons and daughters of the chieftains, flocked to join the nascent monasteries. By the time of his death in 461 Patrick had transformed Ireland, replacing an ancient paganism with a vibrant Church.

In Chartres Cathedral in France, which was built hundreds of years after Patrick, there is a segment of glass in one of the magnificent rose windows. It portrays a group of people, all small in stature, standing on top of each other. Looking at that window, it is said that Bernard of Chartres coined the phrase, 'We are dwarfs standing on the shoulders of giants'. We can all say that in gratitude. But don't let your limitations deter you. Remember that young shepherd boy, Patrick, and what he did. Remember St Paul too: 'There is nothing I cannot do in the one who strengthens me' *(Ph. 4:13)*. And don't forget Malawa. The power of one!

PAUL MIKI
(1564~1597)

In the past, the Irish Church was always keen to remember the penal days, when it was difficult, if not impossible, to practise one's faith in an open way. The centuries of persecution were indeed extremely difficult, and the list of those who paid for their faith with their lives is legion: Oliver Plunkett, Dermot O'Hurley, Patrick O'Healy, Conor O'Devany and many others. Indeed, between 1572 and 1713, we know of many scores of bishops, priests and lay faithful who met a martyr's death.

The Church in its calendar also reminds us that there were other countries that suffered similar fates. Indeed, there has hardly been a single country where the faith is lived and celebrated that has not seen some period of persecution and suffering. We think, for example, of the Uganda Martyrs, the martyrs of Vietnam, and more recently the Jesuits and their housekeepers massacred in the El Salvador conflict in 1989. The list is endless. Each year the Church reminds us of St Paul Miki and his companions, whose feast is on 6 February.

Most people have heard of Nagasaki in Japan. It was there, in August 1945, that an atomic bomb was dropped, killing as many as 40,000 people. A similar bomb had fallen on Hiroshima a few days before. Within forty-eight hours, Japan surrendered, and the Second World War came to an end. The destruction of Nagasaki was ironic in many ways, for it was there that one of the main groups of Christians remained. In one fell swoop, they were almost obliterated. Yet, three and a half centuries before, another attempt had been made to do the same.

When St Francis Xavier arrived in Japan in 1549, he was moderately successful in planting the seeds of faith. Other missionaries followed, and a small Christian community began to grow. Initially, the Japanese rulers were open to the new faith, seeing it as useful to establish contacts with Europe and its rich merchants. But by 1596 things had changed, and Shogun Toyotomi Hideyoshi, the ruler of the country, outlawed Christianity, ordering the arrest of all believers who refused to deny their faith.

The Japanese Catholic writer, Shusaku Endo, in his novel *Silence*, gives an account of the Shogun methods of getting Christians to deny their faith. A missionary might be captured and imprisoned. Rather than torture him to the point of denial, however, the jailers would torture the prisoner in the cell next to his, and tell him that the screaming would stop only if he denied Christ. What a terrible dilemma! Once the missionary had decided to spare his brother his suffering, he himself could no longer go back to the Christian community as a bona fide priest. He had become an apostate. Perhaps it was because of the courage of Paul Miki and his friends, and the lack of success in getting them to deny the faith, that this other method became more popular.

In 1597, twenty-six men were arrested, brought to Nagasaki, and crucified on a hill near the city. Then they were pierced with lances. All of them remained joyful to the end. One of them, the Jesuit Paul Miki, even preached to the crowds gathered beneath the crosses. Here are some of his words: 'The sentence of judgement says these men came to Japan from the Philippines, but I did not come from any other country. I am a true Japanese. The only reason for my being killed is that I have taught the doctrine of Christ. I thank God it is for this that I die. I believe that I am telling the truth before I die. I know you believe me, and I want to say to you all again: ask Christ to help you to become happy. I obey Christ. After Christ's example, I forgive my persecutors. I do not hate them. I ask God to have pity on all, and I hope my blood will fall on my fellow men as a fruitful rain.'

The great early Church apologist, Tertullian, wrote in the second century that 'the blood of the martyrs is the seed of the Church'. How true his words have been in so many ages! Many believed that, with the death of Paul and his friends, Christianity would be finished in Japan.

Not so! The centuries passed, and a more favourable climate returned to the country. Missionaries eventually returned in the 1850s. Some French priests established a mission in the old city of faith, Nagasaki. At first, they did not see any signs of Christianity. Then, one day, they were visited by an old man, who asked them three questions: 'Did they venerate Mary, the Mother of God? Were they married? And did they follow the Pope in Rome?' When they answered to their satisfaction, the hidden Christians of Nagasaki emerged into the open.

Somehow, the Catholics of Nagasaki had lived their faith without priests, as best they could. They had not dared to keep any written materials, but like the early Church, had passed on their faith by word of mouth. The blood of Paul Miki and his friends had indeed fallen on fruitful ground.

The story of a martyr is a story of God's fidelity and his mercy. God, who is faithful, will never abandon anyone. The martyr knows this, and is prepared to let go of his life, trusting he will regain it eternally. God, who is faithful, will not allow the faith to die, but will raise it up in a new generation of believers. The people of Ireland knew this in the centuries of our persecution. The martyrs of Uganda and

Vietnam knew it in the nineteenth century, and the people of Mexico knew it in the twentieth century. The lives and deaths of Ignatius of Antioch, Polycarp of Smyrna, Justin of Rome and countless other early Church martyrs witnessed to Christ by their blood.

Remember to pray for those persecuted for their faith today, about whom we read in the Catholic and worldwide press. We can think of the Christians in Syria, in the Sudan, in Iraq, in Afghanistan or in other parts of the world. Today, in Ireland, persecution no longer leads to the shedding of blood. It takes a different form. May our faith shine through the darkness, just as it did for the Christians of Nagasaki, for God is always faithful and he has promised that those seeds will bear fruit.

PAULINE JARICOT
(1799~1862)

'Little sister, you cannot come; but you shall take a rake, rake in heaps of gold, and you shall send it to me in barrels.' They were prophetic, but painful words, spoken – perhaps unthinkingly – by an older brother to his young sister. He may not have realised how much his words hurt his little sister. He would go on to become a priest on the missions in China. She, too, had hoped for such a missionary enterprise, but instead would answer the call nearer to home. Let us trace the story back to before these words were spoken.

Pauline was the last child of the strong Christian marriage of Antoine and Jeanne Jaricot. Her parents were well-to-do, owning a silk factory in the great provincial city of Lyons. Faith was practised and passed on in her home and, although France was still caught up in the struggles of the revolution which had begun in 1789, the impact was less felt here than in Paris. Pauline was close to her brother Phineas, and often they shared a common interest in missionary stories. One day he confided to her his desire to travel to China and give his life in service of the Lord there. When Pauline spoke of her desire to accompany him, she received a strange word about rakes and barrels, which she did not fully understand until later.

The young industrialist's daughter was introduced early into the hectic social life of the richer families of Lyons. She did what was expected for someone of her rank, attending the balls and fashionable coffee shops, which were part of the sophisticated scene. She attracted many admirers, and for a while she revelled in that milieu. As she found out, however, initially such a life can indeed be intoxicating, but the effects wear off very soon.

Then one day, during the season of Lent 1816, she heard a sermon in her local church on the theme of vanity, and it changed her life forever. The romantic books and love songs, the expensive hair creations, the stylish hats and silk dresses were all laid aside. Pauline began dressing in cheaper clothes, selling her jewellery and giving her money to the poor. Somehow she knew that she was not being called to the religious life, but to live the life of a lay apostle.

Her prayer life became deeper, and she would often spend hours before the Blessed Sacrament in adoration. Indeed, in 1817, she started an association of 'those who make reparation to the Sacred Heart of Jesus'. It was in that same year that, while praying, Pauline had a vision of two lamps. One had no oil; the other was overflowing, and from its abundance oil poured into the empty lamp. To Pauline the drained lamp signified the faith in France, while the overflowing lamp represented the faith of new Christians on the missions. Their faith could revitalise the faith in her homeland.

One evening, while the family were playing cards, she was sitting by the fireside and had another of those ideas for which she was to become well known. 'Circles of Ten', she described her plan as. People would commit themselves to sacrifice a *sou* (roughly a penny) per week; each person would find ten other friends to do the same; and so on. The words about rakes and barrels were beginning to come true.

However, it was in the following year that the seed was sown of what became her most notable achievement. In order to help abandoned babies in China, Pauline appealed to 200 young women and girls who were working in her brother's factory to make a weekly contribution of a *sou* (roughly a penny) from their wages. In that same year, she arranged for the printing and distribution of religious literature. Her idea was that basic religious missionary information should be communicated, and this led in turn to the diffusion of inspiring stories of the missionaries who were in other parts of the world. The seed grew, and in 1822 the Society for the Propagation of the Faith was born.

Another area which grew under Pauline's vision was devotion and prayer to Mary. At the time she felt that the rosary was a neglected prayer. She founded an association called The Living Rosary for people who would pray the rosary and make it better known. Groups of fifteen were organised, made up of all sorts of people: the good, the mediocre and others who seemed to have little to offer but their goodwill. Pauline saw the potential in these groups: 'Fifteen pieces of coal, one is well lit, three or four are half-lit and the rest are not lit at all. Put them together and you have a blazing mass.' In time the organisation would also distribute prayer leaflets, pictures and rosaries.

Yet not all of Pauline's ideas were clothed with success. One *particular* dream came to nothing. She dreamt of creating a Christian town, with a community of workers where men and women would be paid a living wage, everyone would receive a decent education and the sick and elderly would have their needs met. This time, with the advice of the Curé d'Ars, St John Vianney, she gathered around her a group of wealthy people who were each willing to contribute large sums into a common fund. This would be the capital with which she would finance her idea. Sadly, the man to whom she entrusted this capital stole the money. 'You are a victim of fraud', Pauline's lawyers plainly told her.

What was sadder for her was that the association, which she had founded earlier and which had gone from strength to strength, now refused her help. Pauline went back to the Curé who had earlier inspired her original idea. The great French mystic of Ars saw that she was now entering a new phase of her journey to sanctity. His words were full of wisdom: 'Through the hands of the Blessed Virgin, the good God frequently grants one of the greatest gifts – an understanding of the Way of the Cross.' But her life of sacrifice and recent disappointment had taken its toll, and as a result Pauline died in 1862. Her life seemed to end in poverty and failure. Yet she breathed her last words, 'Mary, O my mother, I am yours'.

Pauline was declared Venerable on 25 February 1963. Some months before, in 1962, Pope John XXIII had stated that it was Pauline who 'thought of the Society, who conceived it and made it an organized reality'. Like St Thérèse, the Little Flower, patroness of the missions, Pauline had been unable to set foot in far off fields, but right through her life the missions were in her heart.

PHILIP NERI
(1515~1595)

'*Come stai*? How are you?' the young man would ask. The passer-by would stop, his attention engaged. Then would begin a conversation, which would lead to the usual question, 'Well, brother, when shall we begin to do good?' And Philip lost no time in converting good intentions into action, bringing his 'catch' to visit the sick in the hospitals or to pray in one of the seven great churches of Rome.

Philip Neri, whose feast day occurs on 26 May, would have been at home today in the work of Campus Crusade or taking part in a street outreach project in Dublin or London. His method was direct: like a bee catching the fly with honey, he invited people by the warmth of his personality and by his infectious good humour to stop and chat. But we are not talking about modern evangelism techniques, for Philip lived in the sixteenth century and at a time which was no less critical for the Church than the times in which we live.

Philip was born in 1515 in Florence. Sadly, his mother died when he was young, but a capable stepmother took her place, and Philip himself grew up with a happy disposition, earning the title *Pippo Buono* or 'good little Phil'. After a solid education, he was sent to live with an uncle near the town of Monte Cassino where it was hoped that he would get involved in his kinsman's business. Soon after his arrival, he had a mystical experience – in later life he spoke of it as a 'conversion'

– and he returned to Rome to live by providence alone. Except for the time he spent tutoring two young pupils, he spent much time in prayer in his bare attic. The years of prayer and solitude were followed by a time of study in philosophy and theology, after which he felt ready to launch out on his mission to the people of Rome.

At that time religion was at a low ebb in the city. Rome had not recovered from the devastating invasion of the German and Spanish armies in 1527, a decade earlier. Within the Church itself there were also grave abuses, and although these had long been acknowledged, too little was being done to improve the situation. Luther's protest of 1517 had led to the rise of Protestantism in Germany and beyond. The Sacred College of Cardinals, with a few notable exceptions, were worldly men who thought in terms of power and politics, rather than the service of God and the Church. Indifference and luxury were rife among the clergy, many of whom allowed their churches to fall into disrepair, seldom said Mass and completely neglected their flocks. Little wonder that the laity were lapsing into cynicism and disbelief!

To fill the people of Rome with new ardour, to re-evangelise the city, became Philip Neri's life work. He travelled throughout the city seeking opportunities of entering into conversation with people and leading them to talk about the things that mattered.

Often Philip would engage people at a shop or in the street, indeed wherever he would find them willing to stop and chat. By his warm and personal approach, he gradually prevailed upon many to give up their careless way of life. Then would come the question about doing good, with Philip leading the way for his new disciple.

For ten years Philip continued this work, but in 1548 he felt he needed to formalise his efforts. He founded a congregation called *The Confraternity of the Most Holy Trinity*, whose primary object was to minister to the needs of the thousands of poor pilgrims who came to Rome, especially in years of jubilee. He knew that one such Holy Year was only two years away.

The work extended to looking after the sick, and under his auspices the famous hospital of Santa Trinità was founded. In the Jubilee year of 1575, for instance, no fewer than 145,000 pilgrims were looked after by the hospital.

Initially Philip shied away from the priesthood, but his confessor convinced him that he should be ordained, and in 1551 this took place. Then began a new ministry, that of confessor. Like St John Vianney and Padre Pio in later centuries, he would sit for hours hearing confessions, often telling penitents their sins before they confessed them!

By now others had come to join Philip and the locals called them the 'Oratorians', because they rang a little bell to summon people to pray in their oratory. From small beginnings the congregation grew, and Pope Gregory XIII formally approved it in 1575. By April 1577, work on the *Chiesa Nuova* – 'New Church' – was almost finished. Philip moved to it some years later. Not only did his spiritual sons have free access to him, but his room was constantly sought by others. Rich and poor climbed the steps that led to his refuge at the top of the house.

The Italian people loved and venerated Philip, and visitors even came from other countries to speak with him. In the words of one of his biographers, 'He was all things to all men … when he was called upon to be merry, he was so; if there was a demand upon his sympathy, he was equally ready.'

Two years before his death, Philip retired from his office as superior in favour of his disciple, Caesar Baronius, later to be made Cardinal. He obtained permission from the Pope to celebrate Mass daily in a little Oratory adjoining his room. On the Feast of Corpus Christi, 25 May 1595, Philip was in a radiantly happy mood, and his physician told him that he had not looked so well for ten years. He alone realised that his hour had come. All day he heard confessions and saw visitors as usual. At about midnight, he suffered a severe haemorrhage and the fathers in the house were called to his bedside. Unable to speak, Philip raised his hand, and in the act of benediction passed to his reward. He had reached the age of eighty and his work was done.

His body rests today in the *Chiesa Nuova*, situated in the centre of Rome in a very busy part of the city, where the Oratorians still serve. Six years after his death he was beatified; Pope Gregory XV canonised him in 1622. Pippo Buono loved the Lord and knew so well how to bring others to love and serve him too. It just begins with a smile and a simple 'how are you?'

SATOKO KITAHARA
(1929~1958)

It was Christmas Eve, still a few hours before midnight. The old priest was walking along the quiet country road was lost in his thoughts of the approaching feast. He found it easier to walk away from the busy road, following the trail a tractor had made earlier in the day. Somehow his thoughts strayed back to his years in Japan, to a remarkable woman he had known there.

Hiroshima and Nagasaki are words that immediately conjure up the tragic events of 1945. The dropping of the atomic bombs on these two cities may have brought the war in the East to an end, but it also marked the beginning of a time of reckoning for the Japanese people. As they learned more and more of the war crimes and the brutality of their own soldiers, the people came to realise that their nation had betrayed them. The Japanese code of honour and civility had been severely tarnished. In the aftermath of the bombings, incredible hardship and poverty followed. The poor of the countryside flocked to the cities in huge numbers, cities which were in no position to cope. Many people became disillusioned.

Satoko Kitahara was born in 1929 into an aristocratic family; indeed, in her ancestry she had Samurai warriors and Shinto priests. When the war ended she sought refuge in her studies – her subject was pharmacy – and regained a sense of serenity by immersing herself in them. Yet the quest for a deeper meaning to life was paramount for her.

One day, Satoko happened upon a Catholic church in Yokohama city where she lived. Going inside, she experienced an inner awakening which began to challenge her own inherited beliefs. She discovered a new kind of peace there, and soon sought out the chaplain and some Spanish nuns who were able to answer her many questions. She felt especially drawn to Mary and to prayer. On 30 October 1949 Satoko was baptised into the faith, choosing the names of Elizabeth and Mary.

Soon Satoko met Br Zeno Zebrowski, a Conventual Franciscan from Poland who had accompanied Maximilian Kolbe when he went to Japan in 1930. Zeno had developed a ministry along the Sumida river among the homeless and needy of the area, an area known as Ant Town because of the incredible overcrowding and constant activity there. The people survived by collecting from the garbage dumps and recycling what had been discarded.

Satoko was disturbed. 'I lay down in bed but could not sleep', she recalled later. 'Br Zeno, although unable to read Japanese, had bridged a chasm separating two nations and cultures. He had discovered a part of Japan, less than a kilometre from my home, that I did not know existed. I lived surrounded by carpets and gas stoves, while he went without even an umbrella into the terrible twilight world of destitution.'

Soon she began visiting the area every day, teaching basic grammar, as well as music and hygiene, to the children. Not everyone welcomed her. Two of the local leaders, known as Professor and Boss, who had been raised in Ant Town, resented her presence. 'Why do you come here?' they asked. They were proud that they had been able to help the people of Ant Town to form a community and cling to their only surviving possession – their dignity. They were suspicious of charity and those who offered it.

Satoko too began to ask herself searching questions. 'I thought I was a great Christian because I condescended to dole out some free time, helping the Ant Town children with their homework! Then it hit me. There was only one way to help those children, and that was to become a rag-picker like them.'

It was a radical decision to leave aside her privileged life and to live as one of the outcasts themselves. Soon she too was collecting and selling material, making something of the rubbish others threw away, living as they lived. Her education and innate skills enabled her to organise a room for study as well as a cafeteria. Soon, having negotiated with the city authorities, a classroom and meeting hall followed. Her own devotion to Our Lady gave her the strength she needed for the task. The locals in this Buddhist land even began to call her 'The Mary of Ant Town'.

Over the years, however, the work and conditions took their toll of Satoko's health, and she ended up in hospital. Even Professor came to visit her; she had gained his grudging respect, and he wanted her to return to the town when she was well again. She did – but she experienced a great disappointment there. Her place had been taken by a newly arrived couple, and the dwellers of Ant Town seemed not to have missed her. She felt crushed and alone.

'I will only return', she told Boss and Professor, 'when God calls me.' The two men were impressed. They reflected on her convictions. 'If that God inspired Satoko to help us,' they thought, 'I want to have that God too'. Shortly afterwards both men were received into the Catholic Church, a faith they had once so despised.

There was to be one more miracle for Satoko. For years the city council had wanted to get rid of the eyesore that was Ant Town. They wanted to disperse the inhabitants and redevelop the area. However, they promised that if the people who lived there could come up with a huge sum of money, they would sell them a permanent piece of land. While Professor and Boss and some others went to the city fathers, Satoko prayed. 'Remember, Professor,' she said, 'that years ago I promised to lay down my life for Ant Town. That moment has come.'

When the leaders met with the officials, one of them produced a book Satoko had written years before called *The Children of Ant Town*. It impressed them. They announced that the city would accept a much smaller token payment for the property. Ant Town had been saved. Three days later, Satoko died of the illness she had been carrying for years. She was just twenty-eight years old. She is the first Japanese person to be declared a Servant of God.

The priest continued walking on that Christmas Eve. As he did so, he noticed that the huge tractor wheel had crushed an anthill which had lain in its path. The ants were scurrying about, but without purpose or direction. He thought again of Satoko and the Midnight Mass. He knew he had his sermon.

THOMAS À BECKET
(c.1119~1170)

'Why were you not called Thomas?' the teacher asked. 'After all, you share his feast day.' I could think of no good reason except to say, 'Well, sir, "John" has always been in my family – and I am the firstborn.' Mr O'Duffy was an excellent teacher of English, but his class organisation was … different! His way was to arrange boys in rows, not according to ability or the alphabet, but according to where their saints' names came in the calendar of the Church. So I always sat last in his class at the back in the row furthest from the door.

It was my first real introduction – and one which intrigued me – to one of the several saints whose name is Thomas in the Church's calendar. This was not the apostle who doubted Jesus's resurrection, but the archbishop who resisted a King and paid for it with his life. 'Who will rid me of this turbulent priest?' the King exclaimed at one point. But Thomas wasn't always considered so 'turbulent'!

The life of Thomas à Becket begins in 1118, the son of a sheriff and of Norman descent. His father sent him off to Paris to study canon law. The Archbishop of Canterbury took him under his wing when he returned, and ordained him a deacon. He soon came to the attention of King Henry II of England, and very soon after that he became Lord Chancellor. Life was good for Thomas, and he lived sumptuously, enjoying the friendship of the well-to-do and the glitterati of the court.

Change was afoot, however, when Henry decided that Thomas should become the next archbishop of Canterbury on the death of the incumbent, Theobald. Thomas intimated to the king that things might change if he were to take up this position: 'Should God permit me to be archbishop I should lose your majesty's favour'. Henry was not to be put off, and Thomas was duly ordained a priest and then consecrated as archbishop in 1162.

The king's intentions were not exactly subtle: he wanted 'his man' in the cathedral, a fact that was initially resented by the canons of the chapter. Immediately upon entering office, however, Thomas resigned his office as chancellor. This was not part of Henry's script, but it was a sign that Thomas intended to take his new office seriously. He began fasting and keeping nightly prayer vigils. He even began to wear a hair shirt. Instead of being a patron of actors and a follower of hounds he became 'a shepherd of souls'.

Henry, meanwhile, went on to introduce various reforms in terms of a new code of law and civil administration. But he also wished to go further than any of his predecessors in asserting the jurisdiction of the crown over the Church. This meant challenging the institution of separate ecclesial courts for clergy accused of violating civil laws. It is an issue that has a markedly modern resonance! Thomas stood adamantly opposed to this incursion, for he saw it as an issue of the ultimate authority of the Pope rather than the King. Thomas decided to get offside and retired to exile in a Cistercian monastery in France. He also sought the support of the Pope. The Pope, however, was involved with a struggle with a rival for the papal office and did not wish to antagonise the King of England at this time. There was stalemate, which time and distance helped to maintain.

In July 1170, king and archbishop met on a beach in Normandy and a truce of sorts was effected. Thomas returned to Canterbury, where he was greeted after six years of exile with an outburst of popular joy. But there would be no lasting peace. The underlying conflicts remained. In his Christmas sermon that year, Thomas told his congregation that their bishop might soon be taken from them again.

Within days Henry, in a rage, uttered words which he would later regret, but which sealed Thomas's fate: 'What a set of idle cowards I keep in my kingdom who allow me to be mocked so shamefully by a low-born clerk!' The oft-quoted words – 'Who will rid of this turbulent priest?' – may have been added apocryphally. Four knights understood the king's words of anger, and rode to Canterbury where they found Thomas celebrating evening prayer in the cathedral. They drew their swords and slew him at the foot of the high altar, scattering his brains on the cathedral floor. As he died Thomas said, 'For the name of Jesus and in defence of the Church I am willing to die'.

The martyrdom of the archbishop had resounding consequences throughout Europe. Even in a pre-internet age, news of his death travelled fast and shocked Christendom. Thomas was immediately proclaimed a saint by the ordinary people of England, who were shocked at the treatment of their archbishop. Not everyone might have understood the nuances of the issues for which Thomas died, but the people understood that Thomas had died finally in defence of the principle that there is a higher authority than the King.

Henry himself was forced to acknowledge as much when he fasted for forty days and walked barefoot to the martyr's grave. He even submitted himself to a scourging by the cathedral canons. Thomas was canonised as early as 1173 and his tomb at Canterbury became one of the principal sites of pilgrimage in the whole of Europe. Sadly, the shrine was destroyed during the reign of Henry VIII, but the memory, the witness and the name of Thomas à Becket live on.

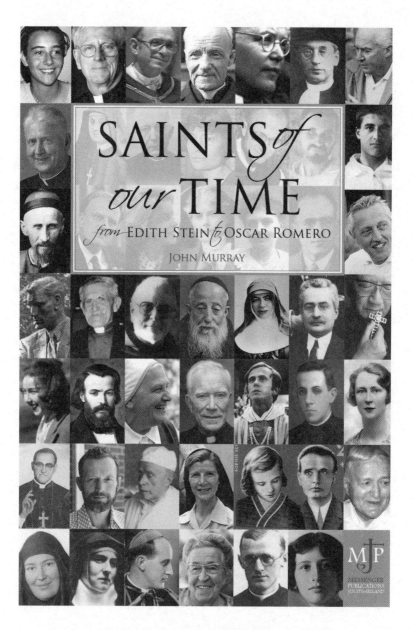

SAINTS *of* *our* TIME

from EDITH STEIN *to* OSCAR ROMERO

JOHN MURRAY

WWW.MESSENGER.IE